Recent Research in Psychology

Shlomo Sharan   Hana Shachar

Language and Learning
in the Cooperative Classroom

Springer-Verlag
New York Berlin Heidelberg
London Paris Tokyo

Shlomo Sharan
School of Education
Tel-Aviv University,
Tel-Aviv, Israel

Hana Shachar
Institute for the Promotion
  of Social Integration in Schools
Bar-Ilan University
Ramat-Gan, Israel

With 7 Illustrations.

Library of Congress Cataloging-in-Publication Data
Sharan, Shlomo
    Language and learning in the cooperative classroom.
    (Recent research in psychology)
    Bibliography: p.
    1. Group work in education—Case studies.
2. Cooperativeness—Case studies.   3. Minorities—
Education—Israel—Case studies.   4. Academic
achievement—Case studies.   I. Shachar, Hana.
II. Title.   III. Series.
LB1032.S454   1988   371.3'95   88-1995

Camera-ready text prepared by the authors using Microsoft® Word 3.0.
Printed and bound by Edwards Brothers, Inc., Ann Arbor, Michigan.
Printed in the United States of America.

9 8 7 6 5 4 3 2 1

ISBN 0-387-96708-7 Springer-Verlag New York Berlin Heidelberg
ISBN 3-540-96708-7 Springer-Verlag Berlin Heidelberg New York

Purpose of This Study

The experiment reported here sought to provide some response to several critical questions that remain unanswered in the research available thus far on the effects of cooperative learning. The salient questions addressed in this study are:

1. Do pupils who study in classrooms conducted with the Group-Investigation method achieve more, academically, in both informational (low-level) and analytic/synthetic (higher-level) kinds of knowledge than pupils who study with the Whole-Class method, or are the effects of the Group-Investigation method on achievement primarily with the latter, not with the former, kinds of knowledge?

2. Is the effect of cooperative learning on achievement more salient for pupils from the majority or minority ethnic groups?

3. Do pupils who study with the Group-Investigation method display more extensive verbal interaction with their peers than pupils who study with the Whole-Class method? Is the spoken language of pupils from the majority and minority ethnic groups affected similarly or differentially by the different instructional methods?

4. Is the pupils' verbal interaction in groups related to their academic achievement?

Abstract

The Group-Investigation method was implemented in 5 eighth-grade classrooms in a junior high school where two-thirds of the student body consisted of pupils from Jewish families who came to Israel from Western countries, and one-third came from countries of the Middle-East. Four other 8th-grade classes in the same school were taught with the traditional Whole-Class method. All eleven teachers of History and Geography in the school participated in this experiment and they were assigned at random to one or the other of the two instructional methods. Teachers of the Group-Investigation classes took part in a series of workshops during the first year of the study, until they acquired an acceptable degree of competence in applying the Group-Investigation method in their classrooms. The experiment proper, encompassing 197 pupils in the classes taught with the Group-Investigation method and 154 pupils in classes conducted with the Whole-Class method, was carried out during the second year of the study.

Two tests of academic achievement (one in Geography, one in History) were administered both before and after the experimental period. Also, 27 groups, of 6 pupils each, were selected at random from the nine classrooms, i.e. 3 groups from each class. There were 3 pupils of Western and 3 of Middle-Eastern background in each group. These groups engaged in two 15-minute discussions (one in Geography, one in History), and the discussions were videotaped. Data about the pupils' inter-ethnic interactions, and about their verbal and intellectual behavior, were obtained from the analysis by two judges of the videotaped discussions.

Results indicate a very superior level of academic achievement by the pupils who studied in the Group-Investigation compared to the Whole-Class method in both Geography and History, and on questions requiring low level (information) and high-level (analytic) answers. The Middle-Eastern pupils received more cooperative statements from all groupmates when they had studied in the Group-Investigation than in the Whole-Class classes. There was a more balanced number of cooperative statements addressed to the Western and to the Middle-Eastern pupils when the discussion groups came from the Group-Investigation as compared to those from the Whole-Class method. In the latter classes, the Western pupils received far more cooperative statements than their Middle-Eastern peers. The same finding, of greater balance between ethnic groups, appeared in the data about the frequency of pupils' speech: Western pupils spoke somewhat less often and Middle-Eastern pupils more often in the groups from the Group-Investigation compared to those from the Whole-Class method. In terms of the frequency with which pupils employed various cognitive strategies in their speech, the Western pupils from both teaching methods performed more or less the same, but the Middle-Eastern pupils derived greater benefit from the Group-Investigation classes. Their speech contained a significantly larger number of such categories than the speech their ethnic peers from the Whole-Class method.

Finally, the data obtained from the discussions were found to relate significantly to the pupils' academic achievement. This indicates that pupil cooperation during small group study predicts a significant degree of their performance on written tests of academic achievement.

These findings were discussed in terms of their relevance for classroom instruction, for different theories of language behavior and language research, and for the issues regarding ethnic relations in the multi-ethnic classroom.

About the Authors

Shlomo Sharan, PhD, is associate professor of Educational Psychology, School of Education, Tel-Aviv University, Israel. He has published books and studies on cooperative learning, and is currently serving as president of the International Association for the Study of Cooperation in Education.

Hana Shachar, PhD, teaches at the Oranim Teachers College, Tivon, Israel, and is on the staff of the Institute for the Promotion of Social Integration in the Schools, Bar-Ilan University. She has many years' experience training teachers in cooperative learning.

This study was made possible by a grant from the Ford Foundation received through the Israel Research Trustees Foundation.

Table of Contents

List of Tables

List of Figures

xv

CHAPTER 1: INTRODUCTION AND BACKGROUND

Academic Achievement

Research on cooperative learning has always addressed itself to both the academic and cognitive effects of classroom instruction on students, as well as to its social-interactive dimension (Sharan, 1980, 1984; Slavin, 1983). The question of the effects of one domain on the other, such as the extent to which academic learning in cooperative small groups is fostered or affected by the pupils' social interaction, has also been raised (Maruyama, 1985). Relating the cognitive and social domains in classroom learning is not easily accomplished because of the myriad constraints upon experimentation in real, ongoing classrooms.

Forty-one studies conducted with various methods of cooperative learning in real classrooms were published up to 1982. These were collected, analyzed and summarized by Slavin (1983). Effects on students' achievement were generally found to be positive, though not in every study and not with every measure. The overall positive effect of cooperative learning versus competitive or individualistic forms of instruction was documented by the Johnson group

1

in their exhaustive meta-analysis (Johnson, Maruyama, Johnson, Nelson and Skon, 1981). Slavin's (1983) review sought to identify critical characteristics of the various cooperative methods that contributed to student achievement in some studies rather than in others. In general, Slavin concluded that "the presence or absence of specific group rewards based on members' learning clearly discriminates methods that increase student achievement from those that do no better than control methods" (Slavin, 1983, 4). However, this conclusion does not apply to the Group-Investigation method. The present study, as well as earlier work with the Group-Investigation method, did not include rewarding students for achievement. The data show that special rewards were not needed to enhance achievement.

High and Low-level Thinking

The study reported here evaluated student academic achievement as a function of cooperative learning experience in two subject areas, History and Geography. In addition to comparing the effects of cooperative versus Whole-Class ("frontal") instruction on achievement in general, this study also sought to determine if these different styles of classroom learning exerted differential effects on children's learning concerned primarily with the acquisition of information (low-level) compared to learning that required analysis of ideas and their application to new problems or situations (high-level). The distinction between low and high-level functioning in the study of cooperative-

2

learning effects stems from the fundamental goal of cooperative learning to create a social environment for pupils conducive to mutual exchange of ideas and perspectives on academic subjects. Typically, in the Whole-Class format of instruction still predominant in most schools, pupils' communication is directed at, or mediated by, the teacher, and is not a part of a communicational network with peers, even though they are physically present in the room. Teacher-centered communication in classrooms allows for students to talk on a one-to-one basis, with different pupils taking turns in talking to the teacher while requiring them to ignore their peers sitting next to them. This form of 'linear' interaction does not create conditions for mutual exchange and clarification of ideas. By contrast, cooperative learning involves much direct verbal exchange among peers who are organized into small task-oriented groups. Hence we hypothesized here that cooperative learning in classrooms would stimulate more higher-level thinking about school subject matter than would Whole-Class instruction.

The hypothesis that cooperative learning in small groups would promote pupils' higher-level learning of ideas than would traditional frontal teaching was examined in two earlier experiments. The first study involved elementary school pupils (Sharan, Hertz-Lazarowitz and Ackerman, 1980). Cooperative learning was found to promote superior achievement on high-level questions (following Bloom's categories) compared to Whole-Class teaching, but no differences were found on questions assessing the acquisition of information. Similar results were reported by the Johnson group in the United States (Johnson, Skon and Johnson, 1980) who also demonstrated that the social interaction within the small groups produced superior problem solving, and that it was not the case that the more able students simply supplied the correct answers to the less able students in the group.

The second study that sought to test the hypothesis of superior high-level learning in cooperative groups was performed in mixed-ethnic junior high schools in Israel (Sharan, Bejarano, Kussell and Peleg, 1984). Classes in English as a second language and in Literature were involved in the study. Student achievement in both subjects was superior in cooperative classes than in Whole-Class learning, but the high-low level of learning was not evaluated adequately. For English-language learning, the high-low level distinction is inappropriate since foreign language acquisition is more a process of learning communicative and linguistic skills than of understanding high level ideas and applying them to novel situations. In regard to the Literature classes in that particular experiment, not all of the teachers in fact taught the same literary works, contrary to their agreement prior to the implementation of the experiment. Hence, only the data from 50% of the pupils, who studied the same materials in both the experimental and control classes, could respond to the same achievement tests (450 out of 850 pupils). Also, the post-test examination was not identical with, and apparently much more difficult than, the pre-test examination, resulting in the fact that achievement scores declined from the pre to the post-test. Due to both reasons of a large 'attrition' rate in the subject population and the difficulty of interpreting the relationship of the post-test versus pre-test scores, the results obtained in that experiment had to be viewed as tentative. With these limitations in mind, the findings from the latter experiment showed that pupils in the Group-Investigation classes (i.e. the cooperative learning method employed in the present study) did, in fact, perform better on questions asking for high-level thinking than did their peers in classrooms conducted with either a Student-Team Learning (STAD) approach or with the Whole-Class approach. Pupils who studied with the two latter methods achieved superior grades on the low-level questions than did those in the Group-Investigation method (Sharan, et al., 1984, pp.65-66).

Achievement in the Multiethnic Classroom

Research on the effects of cooperative learning methods on children's academic achievement in multi-ethnic classrooms was reviewed recently by several authors (Johnson, Maruyama, Johnson, Nelson and Skon, 1981; Sharan, 1980; Sharan and Rich, 1984; Slavin, 1983).

Research on achievement in general in the mixed-ethnic, multi-level classroom, with no special reference to cooperative learning, has also been treated at length in recent publications (Eshel & Klein, 1984; Miller, 1984). Existing research concurs that little progress toward closing the academic achievement gap between majority and minority group children can be expected from desegregation per se. The traditional "frontal" format of classroom instruction is generally considered to be unproductive and inappropriate for the multi-level classrooms that constitute an ever-growing proportion of the classrooms found in public schools today, in many countries. This is certainly true in the United States and in Israel. Moreover, the traditional Whole-Class method actually appears to be an inferior method of instruction for the lower class/minority group pupils in particular who find themselves in "desegregated" classrooms. The social organization of the classroom conducted in the traditional 'presentation-recitation-testing' format, with or without the ubiquitous 'work-sheets' employed by teachers, invites peer competition replete with invidious social comparisons based on social and academic status differences (Cohen, 1984). In such a social setting, minority-group children are largely at a severe academic disadvantage by contrast with their middle-class peers. But the teacher, too, not only the pupils, is at a disadvantage in the multi-level classroom if his/her teaching skills are limited to the Whole-Class method. When the class displays a wide range of abilities and interests, it is patently impossible to reach many of the children with the traditional Whole-Class form of instruction that is based on the assumption that the majority of pupils can and will follow the teacher at the level and pace he/she finds appropriate.

Cooperative learning in the multi-level classroom functions so as to allow for heterogeneity in level of performance, interest and participation within each of the several small groups formed within the classroom.

Together with the redesign of the learning task to allow for within-group collaboration and division of labor, the intimate character and orderly conduct of the cooperative learning group provides each child with the opportunity to contribute to the group's progress and thereby enjoy some academic status among peers while learning (Cohen, 1980, 1987; Sharan and Hertz-Lazarowitz, 1980). Cooperative learning thereby incorporates both the academic and social interactive dimensions of classroom life within the same set of procedures (Sharan, 1980, 1984). In this section we confine our remarks to the achievement aspects of the research. The social, inter-ethnic and language features of this study will be discussed later in this chapter.

In the earlier study of cooperative learning in multi-ethnic junior high schools in Israel, it was learned that pupils from Middle-Eastern background (frequently mis-named as the 'minority' group) derived the same degree of academic benefit from studying in small groups as did their classmates of Western background. No differential effect for ethnicity emerged in the data about academic achievement in learning English as a second language or in the study of literature. Hence, while the 'minority' group children in the cooperative classes achieved distinctly higher scores than did their Middle-Eastern counterparts who studied in classes taught with two other methods, the so-called 'academic gap' was not closed because the Western-background children in the cooperative classes made the same gains (Sharan, Bejarano, et al. 1984, see Table 2.7, page 60).

In his review of the achievement studies with cooperative learning methods, Slavin (1983) cites several reports of race-by-treatment interactions to the effect that lower class/minority-group students in the United States (primarily blacks) displayed larger gains in achievement scores than did white students in the same classes. However, Slavin concluded his review with the observation that the differential effect of cooperative learning methods on lower vs. middle-class (minority vs. majority ethnic/racial groups) was not clearly established. A longitudinal study of the 'activity-centered' classroom on the achievement of Israeli children in mixed-ethnic elementary schools also suggests that learning in cooperative small groups could enhance the achievement of lower-class Middle-Eastern more than of the middle-class Western-background pupils in the same classes (Klein and Eshel, 1980). Again, the data are suggestive but far from conclusive, particularly since the ethnicity effect emerged in the achievement scores on the arithmetic tests but not on the reading tests, a finding that has no theoretical explanation and might prove to be an artifact.

Of relevance for the present study is the conclusion that there is no basis at this time for predicting that cooperative learning will contribute to closing the inter-ethnic achievement gap by benefitting pupils from the 'minority' group more than it will benefit those from the middle-class 'majority' group. We can only hypothesize that it will benefit both groups more than will Whole-Class instruction.

Social Interaction

One of the primary goals of this study was to evaluate the effect of cooperative learning and whole class instruction on pupils' social interaction both within ethnic groups and between members of the two (Western and Middle-Eastern) ethnic groups and/or social classes found in Israel's multi-ethnic classrooms. As such, this was a study of how instructional process affects ethnic-social integration in the desegregated school.

Cooperative learning, from its very onset, has been employed as an educational medium for promoting positive intergroup relations (Cook, 1984; Sharan, 1980, 1984; Sharan & Rich, 1984; Slavin, 1980, 1983). Both the rationale for the application of cooperative learning to the multi-ethnic classroom, as well as the research available thus far on this subject, were presented in the works cited above and will not be repeated here. A recent meta-analysis of all the research findings regarding cooperative learning and intergroup relations provided considerable support for the claim that this approach to school learning does promote more positive ethnic relations (Johnson, Johnson and Maruyama, 1983, 1984; see also Brewer and Miller, 1984).

Close examination of this growing body of research reveals that, with few exceptions, the data documenting inter-group relations in the cooperative classroom were derived from self-report measures. One of the only studies known to these authors that employed a behavioral measure of social interaction as a function of prior

9

experience with cooperative-learning was reported by the first author and colleagues (Sharan, Raviv, Kussell & Hertz-Lazarowitz, 1984). The present study is, in many ways, a replication of this earlier work. One major difference between the previous research and the present study is methodological rather than conceptual, to the effect that the data employed in the present research reflected the total behavior of the pupils during the performance of a group task over a 30-minute period. This was made possible by filming the groups' discussions on videotape. In an earlier study, observers sitting at the table alongside the pupils made two recordings of each pupil's behavior only once every five minutes. Hence, over the same 30-minute period a total of 12 recordings were registered for each child, and the 6-person group generated a total of 72 behavioral acts to be used as data. This quantity of acts is obviously only a fraction of the total number of behavioral events that occurred during the half hour session. The present study aimed at correcting this limitation and the data set employed here was generated by categorizing 100% of the pupils' comments and acts that occurred during the 30 minutes of their participation in a group discussion.

What deserves emphasis here is the fact that the children from the two ethnic groups were also at distinctly different levels of academic achievement and status in their classes. Under such conditions, it was not expected that their social interaction would reveal the symmetrical relations typical of same-status peers (Cohen & Sharan, 1980). We did expect that pupils from the cooperative-learning classroom would display more cooperative and less competitive-oppositional behavior, both within and between ethnic groups, than would pupils from the Whole-Class method. That did not preclude the possibility that pupils from the cooperative clases would still be likely to cooperate with their ethnic peers more than they would be inclined to do with groupmembers from the other ethnic group.

Verbal Behavior in the Multiethnic Classroom

Most of the research available today on the verbal behavior of children that has relevance for the multiethnic classroom was conducted from one of two points of view. One approach investigates children's conversations, often as a function of their age or grade level, while the other approach concentrates on children's language as a function of their ethnic group or social-class membership, comparing the performance of one group to another. No research known to these authors has encompassed both the study of children's conversations and the ethnic or social-class variables as they coincide in multiethnic classrooms. This study yielded information on that topic in addition to our primary purpose of assessing the effects of the two instructional methods on children's verbal behavior in the multiethnic classroom. The entire domain of the effects of instruction on children's spoken language in their native tongue has yet to be given serious attention by psycho-educational research even though speech is the primary vehicle of teaching in most educational settings. Thorough and insightful reviews of language theory and research in schools are found in the work of Courtney Cazden (1986) and Michael Stubbs (1983).

Verbal Interaction Among Pupils

Research on children's conversations sought to illuminate the development of their verbal-communicative abilities. Piaget (1926) was one of the pioneers in this field. He emphasized the notion of egocentric speech that represents an early stage in the development of children's communicative abilities, and the transition to socialized speech. Later studies of children's conversations, that sided either with or against Piaget, contributed to the clarification of the various stages in children's language development (Donaldson, 1978; Dorval and Eckerman, 1984; Gottman and Parkhurst, 1980). Among the topics studied were: the role of disagreement or argument in the development of children's communicative abilities (Genishi and De-Paulo, 1982; Cooper, Marquis and Ayers-Lopez, 1982; Wilkinson and Calculator, 1982), strategies for resolving conflicts among children (Eisenberg and Garvey, 1981), and communicative patterns in groups dealing collectively with academic tasks (Cooper, 1980). Webb (1980, 1982, 1985) studied verbal interaction in groups related to their effort to solve mathematical problems. She classified different kinds of verbal explanations that group members offered to or received from one another. Her findings indicate that the children's achievement scores were related to offering or receiving help during the group's problem-solving effort and if the helpful responses were accompained by an appropriate explanation.

An important contribution to our understanding of how children's conversational abilities develop over the years was made by Dorval and Eckerman (1984). They examined group discussions of children in grades 2, 5, 9, and 12, as well as discussions conducted by young adults up to the age of 30. The study involved 25 groups, five at each grade/age level, and the discussions were analyzed with the use of a list of categories that identified various levels of 'topic relatedness.' The investigators found that young children, ages 7 and 8, are less concerned with sticking to the topic than older children. Questions and answers play an important role in the conduct of the discussion by adolescents and adults but less so among younger children, and the frequency of questions and answers increases with age. As expected, the answers offered in the discussion become more directed to the point of the question as a function of the discussants' age.

The study most analogous to the work reported here was conducted in England by Douglas Barnes and Frankie Todd (1977). They collected 11 hours of tape-recordings made of 56 children in small groups who conducted discussions on topics selected from academic subject matter. The investigators chose to analyze that wealth of material in a qualitative way without reporting the frequencies with which the pupils employed any of their various categories of speech. The report of this study is unique and illuminating. It emphasizes the fact that, given the opportunity, pupils from lower middle-class homes in

13

England will conduct high-level discussions of academic subject matter. The authors pointed out the many benefits to the students derived from this kind of discussion, benefits that were evident in the way the students interacted, both in the social and in the cognitive-intellectual domains. Some of the categories used by Barnes and Todd were adopted by the present investigators, as will be discussed later in this chapter. Due to the absence of quantitative data, it is not possible to transmit here the nature of the findings reported by Barnes and Todd. What bears mention is the fact that the investigators tried to include in their research pupils who typically studied in small groups, as well as pupils from traditional classrooms. But, no attempt was made to observe the classroom instructional practices as they actually occurred, and the authors discovered that the pupils and teachers perceived their classroom experiences very differently. The teachers claimed that they employed small group study frequently while the pupils said that they studied in small groups only rarely. Hence, the investigators abandoned their initial goal of contrasting the speech of pupils from small groups versus traditional classrooms, which is the primary goal of the present experiment. It seems that the Barnes and Todd study reflects the verbal behavior in small groups of pupils who actually had little or no prior experience with cooperative learning methods.

Verbal Behavior of Children from Different Ethnic/Social-Class Groups

A major impetus for the study of minority-group or lower-class children's language behavior came from the need to understand their learning problems in school. Several investigators and theoreticians attempted to explain lower-class and minority-group children's failure in school as related to their use of non-standard and impoverished language (Bernstein, 1971, 1972, 1973; Eiger, 1975; Frankenstein, 1972; Stahl, 1977). Other authors claimed that these children's language was not impoverished but merely different and had its own legitimacy (Baratz and Shuy, 1969; Labov, 1970; Williams, 1970). These two approaches to understanding social-class and/or ethnic-group differences in language behavior are known as the 'cultural deprivation' versus the 'language diversity' schools. Both schools derive their basic concepts from sociolinguistics that concerns itself with the study of the relationship between social factors and language usage (Cazden, 1986; Stubbs, 1983).

Labov (1970) claimed that social class membership exerted much influence on a person's use of formal language structures as representing the use of a more or less standard language code. Bernstein asserted that different social groups express varying kinds of intentions in their language usage, and that these diverse intentions find verbal expression in less formal, more restricted codes that are obviously related to concrete events. Bernstein also asserted that children from the lower social class or from minority ethnic groups employ a non-standard language that is inappropriate for abstract thinking and possesses limited linguistic codes. In short, their language is improverished (Bernstein, 1971, 1973). A succint and critical review of Bernstein's theory (or theories), its serious limitations and problematic relationship with education, is provided by Michael Stubbs (1983).

In Israel an entire literature arose presenting a theoretical basis for the view that minority-group children, mainly from Jewish families who came to Israel from the countries of the Middle-East, have deficient and impoverished language, and, concomittantly, impaired intellectual abilities (Frankenstein, 1972; Minkovitch, 1969; Stahl, 1977). These children reputedly possess a restricted communicative code that implies limited access to the formal expressive capacities of the language, their language includes a high frequenty of cliches and expressions that are dependent on the immediate context and their conversation is very restricted in range and depth. They tend to talk about subjects that appear to be well known to all the participants in the conversation. These features of language and thought allegedly are the consequences of cultural deprivation that hamper these children's capacity for coping with the demands of schooling and the study of academic subject matter. To what extent do lower-class children in Israel, primarily from Jewish families of Middle-Eastern ethnic background, conform to this picture painted primarily by theoreticians and 'clinicians'? Do they in fact display the language features attributed to them?

Stahl (1971) found that there was a gap of three years between Middle-Eastern lower-class children and Western middle-class children in their use of syntax and connecting words. These findings refer exclusively to written, not to spoken, language.

Davis (1977, 1978) did not find any differences between children from the two groups on five measures: 1. The number of abstract terms employed in speech; 2. The number of words denoting causation; 3. The mention of abstract topics; 4. The size of vocabulary; 5. The number of different types of sentences. Both Davis (1977) and Schwartzwald (1981) reported morpho-phonemic differences between members of the two ethnic groups. Schwartzwald found that the lower class Middle-Eastern pupils in her study revealed difficulties in using passive-voice verbs and in forming the future tense of some verbs. Vidislavsky (1984) concluded that, at the time of her study, the existence of a distinct lower-class Hebrew dialect among children from Middle-Eastern ethnic background had not been demonstrated empirically. Hence, there was a need to analyze the syntax and vocabulary in their spoken language. Her data were gathered from 20 pupils aged 16, 10 of Western and 10 of Middle-Eastern ethnic background who were tape-recorded during a 5 to 8 minute interview. The results obtained in Vidislavsky's study support the hypothesis that the two groups speak somewhat differently, with Western students using a more complex sentence structure and a somewhat more differentiated vocabulary (a higher frequency of active content words, and fewer repetitions of the same words). The author concluded

17

that her findings indicated the beginnings of a lower-class dialect, but the data were more in the way of trends that did not constitute a markedly different way of speech. She agreed with Stahl (1971) that the speech of Western pupils was influenced by their reading of written texts, while the spoken language of the Middle-Eastern pupils was much more limited in scope, apparently because its development was influenced primarily by oral language.

Cais (1978) did not discover important differences in the complexity of the syntax in spoken language between children from the two ethnic/social-class groups in Israel. Those differences that did emerge in this study were limited in number. Her study encompassed 72 boys aged 12 years, 48 of whom were from urban middle-class background or from kibbutzim, while 24 were from lower-class background. However, in a more extensive investigation Cais (1984) found noteworthy ethnic group/social class differences in both the quantity and complexity of the children's language. Middle-class girls employed connecting words more frequently than lower-class girls, and lower class children used pronouns without specifying their referent more frequently than middle-class children. Middle-class girls also used the genetive ("construct") form of nouns and made more hypothetical statements than their lower-class peers. Fewer differences were apparent in the speech of boys from the different social classes.

The most extensive and detailed study of Israeli children's spoken language conducted thus far was reported by Shimron (1984). He concentrated on 'referential communication', where one child verbally describes a picture to a second child who is not visible. Again subjects were pupils from Israel's two main Jewish ethnic groups. Middle-class, Western children employed more descriptive-analytic terms, indicating the pictures' structural characteristics. They employed more synonyms and antonyms and used more names for identifying various features of the pictures than their lower-class Middle-Eastern peers from the same grade level (kindergarten, second and sixth grades). It should be noted that many of the differences distinguishing the language of the children from the two groups diminished considerably or were absent from the language of children in the sixth grade by contrast with those in the lower grades.

To the best of our knowledge, the above are the only studies available to date on the spoken language of children in Israel from different social classes/ethnic groups. All of the studies imply that these differences could affect the children's performance in school, but the relationship between language and learning was not investigated directly.

As noted above, another group of investigators views the language of minority ethnic groups or of lower-class children as a different, not deficient, set of communication codes (Baratz and Shuy, 1969; Ervin-Tripp, 1972; Gumperz, 1971; Halliday, 1979; Hymes, 1972, 1974; Mehan, 1980; Stubbs, 1983). In their view, the only relevant criterion for assessing the use of language is whether the individual can communicate with others and understand their language, and not whether the person's language corresponds to the majority dialect. Language should be viewed in terms of its relevance to the cultural context in which it developed where it has its own legitimacy. Cultural subgroups are not linguistically deprived, nor are its speakers linguistically incompetent. All people have an equivalent capacity for language that is complex and potentially creative (Hymes, 1972). There is no basis for the notion of linguistic deprivation in the view of the cultural diversity orientation.

However we are still faced with the fact that the lower-class/minority-group children achieve less in school than their middle-class/majority-group peers. One explanation offered is that the school requires the use of standard language that the lower-class children do not command. In addition, social pressure and prejudice affect the way lower-class or minority-group children are perceived in school that almost determines their eventual failure. Halliday (1979) and Stubbs (1983) maintain that this failure stems from the attitudes toward language that are deeply embedded in the school culture. Teachers transmit to pupils their personal attitudes that clearly convey a message of expectations for and evaluations of the pupils' language performance and ability as distinctly inferior. Halliday argues that schools must enlarge their function in relation to the pupils' language behavior. Language should be treated by schools in terms of its meaning and not in terms of its structure.

It is of interest to note that recently a third school of research on language has been gaining prominence, one that focuses on language as an instrument of communication (Jacobs, 1985). These investigators maintain that the structural and syntactical analysis of language, even the study of its social context, are inadequate for a full understanding of language. Units of analysis must be developed that mediate between the structural and communicative features of language (see a review by Rabin, 1982).

Language Behavior and Educational Policy

In the view of the present authors, all three schools of language described here can contribute to our understanding and education of children in school, in terms of their language behavior. Over-adherence of educational policy to any one of these three schools can result in unfortunate consequences. Thus, adherence to the 'deprivation' position leads to the development of specific curricula for treating lower-class children's language 'deficits' so they acquire the standard dialect, even though, as we observed, it is far from clear that children from lower-class Middle-Eastern background have deficient language. This approach treats lower-class children as 'patients' whose language needs "treatment", and the school program takes on a clinical role (Eiger, 1975). If we adhere to the 'language diversity' school of thought it appears desirable to have pupils in multiethnic classes study textbooks where different language contexts or registers are used so they become familiar with the variety of options available in the culture (Nir, 1976a, 1976b). From the 'language as communication' school one can prepare an instructional program that involves pupils in a variety of

21

experiences that require verbal communication, in order to have them acquire a repertoire of methods for organizing language codes for use in multiethnic settings, both in the classroom and in the wider society (Widdowson, 1978). Littlewood (1981) proposed a communications curriculum that emphasizes the cultivation of language competence, both grammatically and in terms of communicative abilities.

Our position here is that educational policy regarding pupils' language should not rely exclusively on any one of these three schools. The experiment described here, as we have noted before, avoided the use of any particular program focusing on children's language per se. We argue that pupils in school need interactional competencies that include communication with adults and peers and that are sensitive to a complex set of rules and expectations. When the pupils' cultural socialization does not prepare them to employ communication codes that are appropriate for the school setting, their behavior is generally viewed as incompetent rather than as culturally different. The problem for education is to create educational settings that encourage pupils from divergent backgrounds to express themselves fully in the codes they command (Mehan, 1980).

This Experiment and the Study of Children's Language

In one sense, the present experiment afforded an opportunity to evaluate the relative effects of these divergent approaches to instruction, although we clearly did not design the experiment primarily for that purpose. No special curriculum was designed for use in the Whole-Class method aimed at treating the lower-class pupils' language deficits. In this study, the Whole-Class method constituted the educational environment in which most students in school typically find themselves, both in terms of the instructional method employed, and in terms of the multiethnic composition of the classroom which is widespread in Israel today. The Group-Investigation method implemented in this study as part of the independent variable provided a learning environment consistent with the 'communication' and with the 'diversity' orientation toward language behavior. It affords pupils a social setting where they should be able to employ their own communication codes uninhibited by constant monitoring by the teacher. Again, no special curriculum or 'treatments' were prepared to improve the children's language per se. If the communications and cultural diversity approaches are valid, the pupils in this method should demonstrate distinct advantages in their use of language following their experiences in the Group-Investigation classrooms over a period of several months. Higher level language functioning should be demonstrated by pupils from the Whole-Class method if the 'cultural deprivation' model is more relevant, because teachers using this method typically correct pupils' language as they recite, thereby 'treating' their non-standard language usage.

It was not the purpose of this study to investigate the differences in spoken language between members of Israel's different Jewish ethnic groups. However, the data presented here add to our knowledge in that area apropos our primary concern with the effects of two markedly different instructional methods on the pupils' verbal behavior.

The thorough study of children's conversations by Dorval and Eckerman (1984) evaluated the extent to which the discussants at different ages directed their remarks to the topic at hand. It should be emphasized that these discussions had as their sole purpose the goal of getting to know the other discussants better. No particular topic was set by someone outside the group, nor was the time span strictly controlled in any way. Both of the latter features, i.e. a predetermined topic taken from school subject matter, and a uniform time limit, characterized the discussions conducted in the present experiment. Indeed, most of the research on children's conversations assessed spontaneous discourse unrelated to specific topics, whereas the study presented here assessed the effects of specific kinds of school experience on their language behavior. As such, this work differs from much of the psycho- or socio-linguistic research found in the relevant literature today.

Furthermore, the subjects in this study were exposed to one or another of two instructional methods for five months prior to the time their discussions were filmed. In most research on children's language the subjects were not involved in any systematic set of experiences that were thought to exert particular kinds of influence on their language behavior. Also, the two instructional methods employed in this experiment represent two distinct orientations toward children's learning in general, and toward their language in particular. Traditional Whole-Class instruction perceives the children's language as part and parcel of the CONTENT of their academic learning, as a dimension of the subject matter that pupils are expected to learn. Cooperative learning, on the other hand, emphasizes the experiential process in which pupils are exposed to each other's knowledge, ideas, opinions, disagreements, etc.. As part of this process, pupils rethink and rephrase their thoughts and statements until the group concludes its deliberations. This opportunity for thinking and rethinking about one's ideas, and for expressing and rephrasing one's thoughts in conversation with peers, is expected to assist pupils to develop greater control over the functional and communicative aspects of their language repertoire. This complex psychological process unfolds whatever may be the particular character of the linguistic registers, codes or structures that the children ordinarily employ.

Categories of Verbal Behavior: Some Comments on Their Rationale and Background

The verbal behavior of the pupils in this study was classified into 15 categories of speech. These categories were intended to reflect dimensions of interpersonal interaction (six categories) and of cognitive-intellectual functioning (nine categories). To this extent, the present study follows the pattern of research found in a large number of studies on behavior in small groups (see the vast literature reviewed by Hare, 1976). However, almost none of the research available thus far studied pupils' verbal behavior in groups in terms of how they dealt intellectually with the topic being discussed.

A substantial research effort was directed at studying children's language development during infancy when language is first acquired, and many of the categories employed by investigators reflect communicative patterns typical of young children. As one might suspect, categories used to study the speech of children may not be appropriate for use in research with adults. Consequently, many of the categories found in this literature were considered to be inappropriate for use in the present experiment. It can be demonstrated that in the speech of adolescents and adults, unlike the speech of children, the interpersonal interaction is closely related to the topic at hand. In addition to the cognitive demands of a conversation, adult speakers evaluate the topic, attend to taking turns while speaking, and apply this information in order to develop the conversation. That seems to be the primary reason why studies of group discussions that employed category systems for classifying verbal behavior generally did not distinguish between interpersonal communication and the contents of the discussion, which was largely neglected (Smith, 1960; Cooper, 1980). In the Dorval and Eckerman study the quality of the discussion is treated as identical with "topic relatedness."

In the study presented here, we sought to investigate both the social-interactive and cognitive-intellectual features of discussions carried on by young adolescent speakers. Hence, the categories used for classifying the verbal behavior consisted of two sets: One set, called "focused interactions" or "focused turns," has an interpersonal orientation, and a second set of categories, directed at the cognitive domain, is intended to reflect how the pupils dealt with the topic. Focused interactions derive from Piaget's research on children's language, although the categories used here underwent subsequent alterations (Dorval and Eckerman, 1984). Focused interactions are directed toward a specific person for a specific reason in order to obtain immediate results, so that focused interactions have a high level of clarity. However, they do not intend to create opportunities for participation by others.

Not all investigators agree about the role of focused interactions in speech. Piaget believed that these forms of direct communication were part of socially oriented communication, as distinct from egocentric speech, that was found primarily among adults and not among children (Piaget, 1926). Bach and Harnish (1979) proposed a model for conversations where each statement addressed to someone is a kind of "movement" in the direction of the other participants, and where the speaker has clear communicative intentions. Their approach is consistent with that of Piaget regarding the social intention of speech. Other investigators (Hymes, 1972; Rosaldo, 1982) agree that some conversations are organized by clear communicative intentions, but others stem from motives that are not clearly communicative, even among adults. In this study we employed focused interactions as a set of categories that express unequivocal requests and

27

responses, organizational comments (directives) relevant to the conversation, specific agreements and disagreements and comments that interrupted the conversation.

"Directives" (organizational comments) is found in the research literature in a variety of forms. On occasion it is called "instructions" (Cooper, 1980), but more often it was included under the title of "task functions" such as "initiating" (Bales, 1950). In this study, the organizational comments specific to the contents of the discussion were included in the categories of focused interactions ("now it's your turn" or "wait a minute, that doesn't belong to this topic"). Since these basic categories of speech were not employed heretofore in educational research, we cannot predict if their use is subject to influence by children's experience with different instructional methods. Speech patterns do not change quickly. Even the changes documented in the developmental studies are not radical in nature, and they reflect gradual alterations over a period of many years. We are admittedly sceptical about the possibility of changing these patterns of speech during an educational experiment carried out for a few hours a week over a period of five months. These categories were, nevertheless, included in the present study due to their central importance in the research on the development of children's conversations.

The categories of cognitive strategies revealed in the pupils' conversations were selected from a variety of sources, and, in part, they were suggested from the reading of the discussions themselves. Thus, "formulating a hypothesis," "making a statement with evidence," "gives examples," "repeats with expansion," are classes of speech

28

that were used by Barnes and Todd (1977). "Generalizations" was suggested by their category called "categorizing," but it was strongly suggested as well by a reading of the discussions themselves. We were convinced by Barnes and Todd that it is not feasible to evaluate the extent to which the statements made in sequence can be judged for logical consistency or relationship. What makes it difficult to do so is the fact that the logical relationships between statements, even those made by the same speaker, are often left implicit and not formulated explicitly in a way that becomes amenable to external evaluation without conducting an inquiry. Even the speaker may not be able to indicate the precise relationship between one statement and the other. The category of "repetitions" was reserved exclusively for statements relevant to the topic under discussion. This category was adopted from Smith (1960). The category of "repetition with expansion," also confined to facts and ideas directly related to the topic, appears in the study by Dorval and Eckerman (1984) as well as in the Barnes and Todd study.

It is assumed in this study that children who use these cognitive strategies more frequently than other children display a superior form of verbal control of the subject matter. That is not the same as asserting that these categories necessarily indicate a higher stage of thinking in Piaget's sense, i.e. that a higher frequency of some categories rather than others in children's speech testifies to a specific hierarchy of thought. We have no basis for making such a claim. In fact, we are in agreement with Barnes and Todd that "it is not possible to read off a hierarchy of thought from a verbal structure" (1977, page 23). The present experiment concentrated explicitly on verbal behavior as a function of the pupils' experience in classrooms conducted with different instructional methods. We do not know if five months of such exposure changed the children's thought patterns significantly. Nor do we have evidence for identifying the use of these categories in speech with those mentioned in any particular theory that distinguishes lower versus higher levels of thought. That does not mean that schools would not wish to foster children's ability to express themselves in the patterns represented by the categories used in this study. These categories have a high level of face validity, and they appear to characterize a more well-reasoned argument in a discussion. These categories are also found in various theories of intellectual functioning which claim that the inclusion of these categories in verbal behavior makes for more effective communication than their exclusion.

Finally we wish to note that the absence or presence of these categories in the children's speech in no way intends to convey the impression that they are to be considered more or less capable intellectually. This, of course, follows directly from the previous caveat regarding the relationship between these patterns of speech as high versus low levels of thought. What this experiment investigated is the extent to which pupils are able to employ different patterns of speech as a function of their school learning experience, and the extent to which they are free to utilize their verbal powers. It is not justifiable to draw inferences from these data regarding the pupils' mental abilities. The implications of the findings obtained here for the study of language per se must be left to students of linguistics.

CHAPTER 2: METHOD

Population

School

The experiment described here took place in a single school located in the larger Haifa, Israel area. Nine 8th-grade classes of the school's junior-high division participated in this experiment. Many pupils spend their entire public education career in this school that encompasses grades 1-12. Every year the school admits a specified number of pupils from the city's lower-class neighborhoods to constitute 33% of the total number of pupils in all the 7th grade classes. Distribution of the lower-class pupils among the various 7th-grade classrooms is done carefully to ensure their equal representation in each and every class. The other pupils in each class generally come from families of middle-class, or even of upper middle-class, socioeconomic background.

The school has a reputation for its conservative and strict educational orientation regarding the pupils' academic achievement. Discipline receives considerable attention in the school's attitude toward its pupils, and great attention is paid to covering quantities of subject matter at a fairly rapid pace as well as to the evaluation of pupil achievement. Preparation of examinations on each subject is carefully supervised in order to maintain the school's high standards. Teachers invest many hours of work beyond the number of hours in the average work week of teachers in other schools.

Teachers

In five out of the 9 classes in this experiment instruction was in cooperative small groups (Group-Investigation method). Four classes were conducted with the traditional Whole-Class approach. Two disciplines were chosen from the general area of social studies, namely History and Geography. These disciplines served the goals of this particular experiment that was directed, inter alia, at assessing the effects of cooperative learning on children's language behavior in multi-ethnic groups.

A total of 11 teachers, constituting all of the History and Geography teachers in the school, participated in the study, and they were assigned at random to either the cooperative learning or Whole-Class method, 6 teachers to the former and 5 to the latter method. Nine teachers attended a series of workshops, 6 who were to teach the cooperative learning classes, and 3 of the 5 teachers who were intended to teach with the Whole-Class method. The latter 3 were asked to learn the new method, even though they were not to implement it in their classes. This was done in order to check the pupils' achievement for possible improvement as a function of their teachers' participation in the workshops without directly implementing their new skills.

Students

The subjects in this study were 351 students in the 8th grade, 197 of whom were in classes conducted with the Group-Investigation method, and 154 were in the classes taught by the traditional Whole-Class method.

It should be noted that the lower-class pupils were largely from families who came to Israel from the Moslem countries of the Middle East, while the middle-class pupils were primarily from families of Western background (Europe, North and South America, South Africa, etc.). The educational background of the pupils' parents, by instructional method and ethnic group, appear in Table 1 (see page 35).

In-Service Teaching Training

Teaching training to develop skills in cooperative-learning in small groups through the Group-Investigation Method was carried out in a series of 10 workshops, each lasting approximately 3 hours. These workshops were devoted to the following topics: 1. The basic principles of cooperative learning; 2. Techniques for training pupils to conduct small-group work; 3. Developing children's communication and listening skills; 4. How to train pupils to plan, both independently and collectively, a study project; 5. Pupils' independent use of learning resources; 6. How to

Table 1

Ethnic and educational background of parents of pupils in Group-Investigation (N = 197) and Whole-Class (N =154) methods (number and percentage).

Western (N = 236)

Method		Higher Educ.		High School		Elementary	
		Father	Mother	Father	Mother	Father	Mother
Group-Investigation	#	100	93	24	25	13	6
	%	51	47	12	13	7	3
Whole-Class	#	60	49	30	26	9	9
	%	39	32	20	13	6	6

Middle-Eastern (N = 115)

Method		Higher Educ.		High School		Elementary	
		Father	Mother	Father	Mother	Father	Mother
Group-Investigation	#	7	4	26	25	26	29
	%	4	2	13	13	13	15
Whole-Class	#	3	3	29	25	24	29
	%	2	2	19	16	16	19

35

help pupils prepare and present to their class reports of their group study projects.

The educational principles and classroom procedures for implementing the Group-Investigation approach to cooperative learning were presented in several publications and will not be repeated here in detail (Sharan and Hertz-Lazarowitz, 1980; Sharan and Sharan, 1976). A short overview of the six stages of the Group-Investigation method conveys some of the flavor of this approach and the extent to which it differs radically from Whole-Class instruction by the traditional presentation-recitation method.

The six stages are:

Stage 1. Identifying the Topic and Organizing Pupils into Groups (Classwide)
Students scan sources, propose topics and categorize suggestions.
Students join the group studying the sub-topic of their choice.
Group composition based on interest and is heterogenous.
Teacher assists in information gathering and facilitates organization.

Stage 2. Planning the Learning Task (in Groups)

Students plan together:
What do we study?
How do we study? Who does what? (Division of labor.)
For what purpose or goals do we investigate this topic?

Stage 3. Carrying Out the Investigation

Students gather information, analyze the data and reach
   conclusions.
Each group member contributes a share to group effort.
Students exchange, discuss, clarify and synthesize ideas.
   Team - building exercises are used as necessary to
   sustain productive participation by students in their
   groups.

Stage 4. Preparing a Final Report

Group members determine essential message of their
   project.
Group members plan WHAT they will report and HOW they
   will make their presentation.
Group representatives meet to coordinate plans for final
   presentation.

Stage 5. Presenting the Final Report

Presentation made to the entire class in a variety of forms.
Part of presentation should actively involve the audience.
Audience evaluates clarity and appeal of presentation
   according to criteria determined in advance by the entire
   class.

Stage 6. Evaluation

Students share feedback about the topic, about the work
   they did and about their affective experiences.
Teachers and pupils collaborate in evaluating student
   learning.
Assessment of learning should evaluate higher-level
   thinking.

Teacher workshops were conducted with a wide range
of instructional techniques, including the viewing of closed-
circuit television films for training teachers in cooperative
learning (Sharan, Lazarowitz and Reiner, 1978),
simulations, small-group work with colleagues on topics
related to the goals of the workshops, cooperative planning
of classroom procedures for cooperative learning,
formulating instructions for pupils, and reporting on one's
group work to the class (of teachers). Toward the end of the
series of workshops, teachers were asked to prepare a unit
of study in their subject and to try it out in their classes, with
supervision from one of the investigators (Hana Shachar).
Some of the teachers reported that their pupils were able to
present very interesting reports to their classes after they
had completed a group study project.

During the course of the workshops, two distinct trends
could be discerned among the teachers. The new group-
centered teaching method constituted a near-revolutionary
upheaval in their teaching concepts and repertoire, as the
teachers themselves testified on several occasions.
Despite the great change in behavior demanded by the

new method, the teachers displayed considerable devotion to the training program and participated with a high level of interest and motivation. It seems that the norms of high-level professional involvement typical of this school's tradition influenced the teachers' response to this experiment even though it aroused conflicts in the teachers' attitudes.

Implementation

The in-service training program and the teachers' initial trials in applying cooperative learning in their classes occupied the first year of the project. At the onset of the new academic year, the 11 teachers met twice in two groups - one group for History, the other for Geography - to delineate the precise contents of three study units in each subject area that would be taught for a specified period of time during the new year. This period was designated as the 'experimental' period, with measures to be taken toward its conclusion (for social and verbal behavior) or both at the start and conclusion of a given study unit (for academic achievement). A timetable was set up jointly by the cooperative-learning and Whole-Class teachers to be observed by all teachers so that each study unit would be taught for the same number of sessions in all 'treatment' classes. This was necessary not only to ensure that both styles of learning would devote the same amount of time to each study topic, but also to determine the uniform nature of the contents so that all teachers would emphasize the same topics.

In the cooperative-learning classrooms, each pupil was a member of a 4-person group that served as the social unit for learning purposes. Groups were composed by selecting pupils at random from among those who expressed an interest in a given sub-topic of the subject under study. Each unit of study lasted 6 to 10 weeks, depending upon the nature of the topic, and all the 4-person groups in each class were reshuffled after each unit. Group composition was also modified by teachers' judgements about the extent to which group membership represented, as far as possible, a cross-section of the class membership in terms of academic status, ethnic background and gender. In no instance were the groups that were formed for the purpose of being videotaped identical with those that existed during the implementation of the experiment.

Classroom Observations

A series of systematic observations were carried out in all classrooms to document the nature of the teachers' instructional behavior and to ascertain if this behavior embodied the principles of the two teaching methods. It was also necessary to ascertain if the teachers intended to employ the Whole-Class approach, who had participated in the cooperative-learning workshops, had changed their behavior, contrary to the plan of the experiment. Two observers were trained to carry out these observations with the help of structured observation schedules appropriate for each of the two teaching methods. These observers were trained for this task with the use of pre-recorded videotapes, and by practicing in real classrooms, until they reached a level of 94% of inter-rater agreement in their observations.

The observers entered each class twice at the onset of the experiment before teachers began to participate in the cooperative learning workshops. This was done in order to document the teachers' Whole-Class instructional behavior. It was found that 68.2% of the total teacher-pupil communications occurring during the period of observation (2 class sessions) consisted of teachers' short questions intended to elicit short answers from the pupils at the level of bits of information, while 22% of the communication dealt with teachers' efforts to impose discipline on the class. No communication whatsoever reflected a pupil-centered rather than teacher-centered form of classroom social structure. Hence, there were very few instances of teachers organizing inter-pupil discussion or exchange or providing an opportunity for pupils to speak to each other. The mean percentage of such events was 4.2%, with a range of 0-6%.

Two more observations were conducted in all classes toward the end of the first study unit, i.e. about 6 weeks after the experiment had begun, and two additional observations in the classes of the 6 teachers who taught with cooperative small groups. These data show that no real change occurred in the way teachers conducted lessons when they used the Whole-Class approach, even those teachers who experienced the cooperative-learning workshops (70.1% short questions; 21.2% disciplinary remarks; 4.9% more 'liberal', i.e. pupil-centered communications).

Another important finding from the observations was the number of pupils in each class, out of a total of 40 pupils exactly per class, who spoke during a typical frontal lesson. On the average, 16 out of 40 pupils participated in a given lesson, with a range of 10-22 pupils. Of these, only an average of 5 pupils in each class spoke more than 4 times during the course of a lesson. This rate of pupil participation did not change from the first set to the later set of observations.

A marked change in interaction patterns occurred in the cooperative learning classrooms. Disciplinary remarks by teachers declined by 36% (i.e. from 22% to 14% of the total teacher-pupil communications). Teachers' short questions to elicit short replies from pupils declined from 69% to 11%. Peer communications occupied the bulk of the communication transpiring in the classroom.

Dependent Variables

Pupil Academic Achievement

Pupil achievement in this experiment was assessed for one out of the three study units in History and for one unit in Geography, both before and after the study of the given unit. The examinations were composed jointly by the teachers in both the cooperative learning and Whole-Class methods. In all of the examinations, half of the items were formulated to elicit answers at a low-level of intellectual functioning, following Bloom's taxonomy (i.e. information, description, understanding) and the other half of the questions were directed at eliciting high-level responses involving analysis, taking a position regarding an issue, dealing with hypothetical situations related to the subject area, etc.

The History examination consisted of 8 questions (4 Low-level, 4 High-level) and the Geography test had 14 questions (7 Low- and 7 High-level).

Several considerations dictated the need to limit the number of questions on the examinations. It was necessary to allow pupils to complete each examination during one 45-minute class session. A team of 4 teachers estimated the amount of time a pupil would need to answer each question. They determined that 8 questions in History would require 45 minutes if 4 low-level questions required 4 minutes per question (16 minutes) and 4 high-level questions required 7 minutes per question (28 minutes). A similar pattern was followed for Geography: Teachers estimated each low-level Geography question as requiring 2 minutes to answer (14 minutes), and 4 minutes for each high-level question (28 minutes).

After the initial formulation of the questions by a team of 3 teachers in each of the two disciplines, including the school subject-matter coordinator for that discipline, both tests were given to two senior teachers of that subject from a different school. These 4 judges (2 for each subject) were asked to categorize the questions as Low or High level, in light of Bloom's criteria. These judges reached 96% agreement regarding the level of the questions formulated by the teachers.

Here are several examples of test questions at different levels:

History (low-level): What do you know about Rabbi Yehuda Ha-Levi?"

Geography (low-level): "Explain the term 'megalopolis.' "

History (high-level): "If Maimonides would appear today in Israel, which current problems of Israeli society would you care to discuss with him? How do you think Maimonides would relate to these problems"? Base your reply on your knowledge of Maimonides' ideas.

Geography (high level): "Can you compare New York and the Megalopolis to Tel-Aviv and the cities of the Dan district in Israel?" Explain!

Scoring

Evaluation of responses to the items on the Geography test was constructed so as to allow for a possible range of scores from 0-7, with a chance of receiving an additional 2 points for an outstanding reply to two of the questions. This would result in a total range of 0-98 points on the Geography test. In History, each question could receive a range of 0-12 points, so the range of scores for the total test in History was originally 0-98.

Two teams of 3 teachers each (one for each subject) determined the exact criteria for scoring pupils' responses to each question on each test, in order to establish uniform criteria for judging when a response is to be evaluated with

44

a given number of points. These criteria were recorded in writing.

The 'experimental period' for the purpose of evaluating achievement in this experiment was 2 1/2 months, and both tests (History and Geography) were administered twice, just before and soon after the conclusion of that period. It should be noted that the particular unit under question was taught during the months of December to February. This timing of the experimental period was crucial because it was imperative to allow several months' time at the beginning of the academic year for teachers to accustom the students to working together cooperatively in small groups. The point of the research portion of this study was to assess the effects of cooperative small group learning on various dependent variables. Such assessment would be unreliable if the evaluation would take place at a time when the students were still acquiring the basic skills of group study and adjusting to the marked change in their long-standing expectations and habits. The need to allow students time to adjust to the new procedures parallels the need to retrain teachers in group skills and to allow them to acquire confidence in their use. The teachers in this experiment had over 6 months' time to learn the new method and to change their professional attitudes and habits. At least three months' time had to be devoted to having students absorb the meaning of the change they experienced before any assessment of the educational products would be legitimate. In sum, the pupils studied two instructional units in each of the two subjects in cooperative small groups over a period of three months prior to beginning their study of a third unit. It was on their knowledge of this latter unit only that their achievement was evaluated in this study.

The examinations in each subject were scored by one teacher, and then given to a second teacher for reliability. Few differences were found between the two scores, primarily, it seems, because of the care that had been taken in establishing unambiguous scoring criteria by the teams of teachers prior to the scoring effort. All personal identification of the pupil was removed from the test booklet so the teachers who marked the examinations could not discern the pupil's identity or in which class the pupil had studied. The test booklets did not have the pupils' names in them and, hence, could not be associated by the teachers who scored them with pupils who were in the cooperative or Whole-Class method.

Before the achievement data were analyzed statistically, the distribution of pupils' scores on each question was calculated and examined. This procedure revealed that two questions on the Geography test (both High-level) and one on the History test (also High-level) were probably very difficult and were not answered by a large number of students in both the cooperative and Whole-Class groups. These three items were eliminated from the statistical analyses. Consequently, the ranges of possible scores on the two achievement tests were as follows:

History		Geography	
Low Level:	0-44	Low Level:	0-41
High Level:	0-36	High Level:	0-39
Total Test:	0-80	Total Test:	0-80

Middle-Eastern/lower class and Western/middle-class pupils were not evenly represented in the two instructional methods. Hence, the effect of parental education on achievement was statistically controlled by using father's level of formal schooling as a covariate. The achievement data were analyzed in two ways. First, a split-plot design analysis of covariance with unequal Ns was used, with the treatments (Group-Investigation vs. Whole-Class teaching) as a between groups factor and classrooms were nested in treatments, the pre- and post-test scores were a within-group factor, and father's education was a covariate (see Appendix). A second set of analyses used individuals' achievement scores in a 2x2x2 split plot design analysis of covariance with the two teaching methods and ethnic groups (Lower-class/Middle-Eastern vs. Middle-Class/Western) as between-group factors, pre- and post-test scores as a within-group factor, and father's education as a covariate.

Videotape Films of Pupils' Behavior

Data about the pupils' social-interactive behavior, and about their verbal behavior, as a function of having participated for several months (about 6) in cooperative learning or in Whole-Class styles of instruction, were gathered by the use of videotape films. In this way only is it possible to obtain a total record, rather than just a sample, of behavior that is subject to careful control as well as unbiased in its completeness.

In each of the 9 classrooms that participated in this experiment teachers were asked to compose 3 groups of 6 pupils each to be filmed on videotape while performing a task that is uniform for all groups. The groups were to be composed at random, but with 3 students selected from those of the Western middle-class background, and 3 students from among the Middle-Eastern/lower-class background students in the class. Teachers were also asked to maintain a gender balance in each group if possible, as well as a distribution of pupils from different levels of academic achievement to avoid having groups comprised primarily of high or of low achievers. Obviously, comprising three groups that meet all of these criteria, out of a class of 40 pupils, is a complex task.

In light of the above we wish to recall the fact that there were a total of 351 pupils in this study in both the co-operative and Whole-Class methods in a total of 9 class-rooms. Most of these pupils responded to the academic achievement tests. However, for the purpose of studying the effects of the teaching methods on pupils' social and language behavior, we formed approximately 3 6-person groups in each class, half of the pupils from Western/middle-class homes, half of them from Middle-Eastern/lower class homes. These groups were videotaped. A total of 179 pupils participated in these groups. This number resulted from the fact that, despite our plan to have the exact same group appear in both the History and in the Geography groups, some pupils were absent at the time of filming, and in most, but not in all cases, another child had to be substituted for the one who was absent. Of the 179 pupils, 86 came from cooperative-learning classes, and 93 from Whole-Class instruction. There were a total of 29 groups videotaped, 2 of whom had 5 members. Six groups had one child absent in one or another session, so that a replacement was required. There were 27 groups of 6 pupils who appeared in both filming sessions.

The videotaping of the group interaction took place in a special room in the school, not in the regular classroom. It was imperative to separate the filming process from the classroom to avoid both the distractions and the noise-level of the regular class. Also, the camera equipment had to be left in the same position for several weeks until all the groups had been filmed twice, once while engaged in discussion of a task taken from the History course, and once a task from Geography. Each task, with identical group composition, was filmed for exactly 15 minutes. No group was filmed twice on the same day. First, all the groups discussed the History task. Only when this wave of filming was complete were the groups invited a second time to discuss the Geography task. Each group was given several minutes 'warm-up' time before the actual filming began.

The technicians operating the two cameras in the room - to film two groups simultaneously - were instructed not to move the cameras and not to focus them on any particular child. The frame was to include all 6 pupils at all times, so that the observer would be able to determine not only <u>who</u> was speaking but <u>whom</u> the speaker was addressing.

Pupils coming from classes taught with the Whole-Class method were not accustomed to participating in peer discussion groups. In order to avoid having the filming session come as a surprise and a novelty to them, the teachers of the Whole-Class method were asked to conduct two 15-minute discussions with the 6-person groups in their classes prior to the film session. In this fashion, all the students from the 'control' classes were exposed to a group discussion situation before they were filmed, despite the fact that this kind of experience is distinctly <u>not</u> part of the usual Whole-Class teaching method.

<u>Group tasks</u>: The History and Geography topics given to each of the groups to discuss were typed on a page and given to each group before filming began. Each page contained instructions plus one topic for discussion. The History instructions were:

50

1. Please read the following selection.
2. This selection raises a question that concerned the Jewish community throughout the centuries of Exile up to this very day. That question is: Is it important to maintain our unique character or to integrate completely into the society where the community lives?

   a. Discuss this question among yourselves and express your opinions about maintaining separate identity or integrating. Please explain the reasons for your opinions.
   b. Think about whether this question applies to our time as well. Give some examples to illustrate your position.
   c. Let us assume that your group would be asked to serve as a team of advisors at a Zionist Congress and to plan a discussion of the question about the separateness or integration of the Jewish community. What specific points would you recommend for discussion, and what direction would you give to the discussion? Record your suggestions in writing.

The Geography instructions were:

Check the atlas to determine the location of the large concentrations of population in the United States, and explain their existence in these places.

1. Give several reasons why populations are concentrated in those areas. Record your reasons.
2. What consequences result from the concentration of such large populations?
3. Assume that your group is asked to advise the American Government. Would you recommend that it adopt a policy of population dispersion? Discuss and explain your recommendations and summarize them in writing.

Both topics were intended to relate pupils' knowledge to their life experience and to avoid having them depend exclusively on knowledge acquired in school. Such tasks hopefully would allow the less able students to express their opinions as well and not have the discussion monopolized by the more able students.

Scoring the Films

The films were scored for the frequency and quality of the students' social interaction, language behavior and cognitive strategies evidenced in the discussion. Three judges were trained to score the films, none of whom had taken any part in this experiment or had any knowledge of which pupils belonged to the Group-Investigation or Whole-Class groups.

The judges received a list of categories about the social, verbal or cognitive strategies of the pupils. Their task was to categorize all of the events occurring in each 15-minute discussion that were relevant to a particular set of categories. Two judges worked individually, each on a separate set of categories (social interaction or verbal-cognitive behavior), and a third judge categorized films selected at random for the purpose of ascertaining inter-rater reliability, that was found to be .93 for the social categories, and .90 for the verbal-cognitive categories.

Mehan (1979) has written eloquently and insightfully about the limitations on the study of classroom interaction inherent in the use of preplanned category systems. In particular, systems of categories for quantifying children's speech in school obscures the "contingent nature of interaction" and ignores the context, hence the meaning, of the speech as it occurs. Mehan is doubtlessly correct in asserting that a sequential, rather than categorical approach to the study of verbal interaction is needed to provide an adequate ethnography of classroom life. We must emphasize that even the results of painstaking ethnographic investigation are contingent upon the character of classroom instructional methods and processes, and are not only a function of the participants' linguistic capacities. Also, the present study sought to document some of the differential effects on children's use of language exerted by distinctly different instructional methods and processes. We did not seek, in the present study, to document the nature of the verbal interchanges that occur during the unfolding of those instructional methods in the classroom. In short, this study reports some effects on children of having studied in one versus another kind of classroom, when some of the classroom events follow different models of teaching, rather than providing a microanalysis of how the different teaching models were actually reflected in classroom speech patterns. With all these comments about the pros and cons of different methodologies for the study of language in the classroom, the present authors hope in the future to subject the videotaped discussions of the 27 groups of 6 pupils each to a detailed analysis that will focus on the context and meaning of the children's talk.

Behavioral frequencies were recorded for each pupil in each group. Pupils in each group were numbered for identification, and the same seating order was maintained in both 15-minute filming sessions. Pupils' ethnic/social class identification was made from a master list not available to the judges.

The first step in scoring the films was to transcribe all the verbalizations so that the judges would have a written text to compare with the film. The films were transcribed by repeated viewings so as to be as complete as possible.

During the initial viewing of the films, several obstacles to scoring were recognized. Pupils spoke simultaneously, making it difficult to identify the contents; a pupil turned his/her back suddenly to the camera; sudden movements were made away from the microphone; someone turned their head away from the camera. Such instances required repeated viewings until everything could be recorded.

Viewing was subdivided into sections of several seconds in duration only, in order to make the quantity of events to be evaluated manageable. In this fashion both the identity of the speaker and the speech could be recorded, at least after several repeated viewings (usually 3 or 5). Very few words or sentences could not be deciphered after several repeated viewings.

Categories of Social Interaction

The social-interactive behavior of the pupils in the 6-person groups, as videotaped, was analyzed according to the following categories:

1. Cooperation (Positive Social Behavior)

   a. Task-oriented cooperation: This includes both verbal and non-verbal behavior directed at solving some problem to achieve the collective group goal. These behaviors include exchange of ideas and information, suggestions and opinions related to the task. Examples would be: When someone asks a task-related question and gets an appropriate answer; expressing an opinion that results in a relevant reply from a member of the group or when the opinion is accepted by the group; reinforcing someone's comments or praising them.

   b. Socially-oriented positive behaviors: These behaviors were not directly related to the group task, and they reflect expressions of empathy, or support for other group members. For example, saying "Ronnie wanted to say something," or transferring the microphone to someone, or saying "Every time Yossi tries to talk someone interrupts him, let's give him a chance now."

55

c. Listening in order to respond: This refers to an act of listening closely followed by a response, verbal or non-verbal. The response includes agreement or disagreement, and is distinct from passive listening that is not followed by any contribution to the group.

2. Lack of Cooperation (Negative Social Behaviors)

   a. Competition: There was little competition possible in these films in the sense of pupils pursuing individual goals exclusive of others. Rather, the operational definition of competition employed here referred to a pupil's attempt to have his/her ideas or suggestions receive a primary place in the group's discussion. For example: "I'm right, what you said is plain nonsense." "Oh shut up, I want to summarize what we said."

   More precisely, this category included verbal attacks on others, ridicule, aggressive remarks or acts. Examples are: A pupil rejects someone's suggestion (not merely expresses opposition per se, but rejects an idea on substantive grounds); expresses something unpleasant causing another pupil to be confused or put out; a pupil seeks to attract attention or demonstrate superiority; mocks others' ideas; interrupts the group's activity by making noises or sounds.

b. Opposition: This occurs when someone objects to what another student said in a way that does not contribute to the group but primarily expresses opposition. Some manifestations of opposition possess positive character and constitute a contribution to the group. Such behaviors were classified as cooperative task-oriented behavior. The category being discussed here is negativistic, such as: "You're all wrong. Listen to what I want to say. Look at the map. It's not like what you said. You're wrong."

c. Criticism: This type of interaction is very similar to category 2b (opposition). In addition to opposition, this type of expression has a judgemental element about the other person or his/her behavior, and does not only express opposition. "You're just talking nonsense. That's not right. You're just saying that because you didn't hear what we had said before." "You're behaving like a baby. Just look at what you're doing."

3. Individual Behavior

a. Task-oriented individual behavior: This includes all acts made by a group member to progress independently toward solving the group problem, such as examining the text (atlas) for a long time, without being involved in the group discussion.

b. Individual behavior not related to the task: Refers to all acts in which the student engages alone without reference to other group members or to the group task. Students could watch the camera, doodle on paper, whisper to others, etc.
c. Confusion: Appears removed, seems to day-dream or is otherwise distant from the group activity.

4. Cooperative Acts Directed at the Group

A pupil addresses a positive statement to the group as a whole and not to any particular group member.

The basic unit of analysis for recording pupils' speech acts was a complete 'turn', i.e. an opportunity used by a student to speak. When a 'turn' was long so that it consisted of several sentences, it was possible to apply the system of categories to the analysis of the speech-acts. Occasionally the speech acts expressed during a given 'turn' contained more than one verbal category.

Categories of Verbal Behavior

Three sets of data were derived from the analysis of the pupils' verbal behavior.

a. The Frequency of Speech
The first set concerned the frequency of the pupils' speech without regard for structure or content, namely: how many words did the pupils employ each turn they took in

speaking, and how many turns did pupils take during the course of the 30 minutes of discussion in the 6-person groups? A pupil's turn at speaking was considered without reference to the length of speech or its content. When a pupil stopped speaking on his/her own initiative, or when the pupil was interrupted, that constituted the end of a turn. If the pupil continued to speak after an interruption, the continuation was counted as a new turn. This definition of a turn is widely used in current research (Dorval and Eckerman, 1984; Cherry and Lewis, 1976; Feldstein and Welkowitz, 1978; Garvey and Berninger, 1981; Sacks, Schegloff and Jefferson, 1974). In instances where the speech of two pupils occurred simultaneously, the speech of each pupil was scored separately.

b. Focused interactions

The categories of focused interaction employed in this study are almost identical to those used by many investigators of children's language ever since the work of Piaget (see Dorval and Eckerman, 1984). However, these categories as well as those reflecting the pupils' cognitive strategies were all derived empirically from the data gathered in this study. Transcriptions of the group discussions were read independently by 2 judges. After reading a given section, the judges discussed their classifications and their points of disagreement. Categories about which they could not agree, after this entire process was concluded, were eliminated. Only 2 categories were discarded in this fashion, and the definitions of 3 other categories were changed. Inter-rater reliability for the classification of the pupils' statements was .94.

The categories of focused interaction used in this study are:

1. requests for clarification; 2. gives clarification; 3. agreement; 4. disagreement; 5. directives (organizational comments, and 6. interruptions. Categories 1, 2, 3 and 5 can be combined into a scale of 'positive focused interactions.'

'Focused interactions' are defined as a turn of speech aimed at imposing the speaker's intention on the conversation for a specified purpose and directed at a specific listener (Austin, 1962; Searle, 1969, 1979). Thus, focused interactions have a distinct social meaning. The six categories of focused interactions are defined as follows:

1. Requests clarification (asks questions). These acts refer to those questions that one pupil addresses to another to obtain information about what the other pupil had said.

Example: "Give some example of what you said before." "What are the social ideas of religion?"

2. Gives clarification. This is every reply offered by one pupil to another (or to others) that refers directly to a request for clarification made by another pupil.

Example: "There is variety in all kinds of ideas, not only in people." "What we're talking about is whether in Spain it was better to integrate."

60

3. Agreement. A response of agreement to a statement made by another pupil.

4. Disagreement. Again, in response to another pupil.

5. Directives. A directive is any comment concerning procedures for the conduct of the group discussion.

Example: "OK: let's begin. "Let's take Siberia, for
             example....
             "So we all reached the conclusion that...."

6. Interruptions. Whenever one pupil injected a comment while another student was talking.

Piaget (1926) considered focused interactions to be crucial features in the development of socialized speech. Recent research does not always agree with this view (Dorval and Eckerman, 1984). Nevertheless, these categories are generally acknowledged to constitute the fundamental substructure of conversational communication.

c. Cognitive strategies

The third set of data about the pupils' verbal behavior concerns the cognitive-intellectual features displayed in the discussions. The cognitive strategies are more content-oriented than the categories of 'focused interactions,' although the cognitive strategies revealed in the pupils' speech do not treat the actual substance of the discussion. These features describe how pupils used the language rather than what they said about the subject they were asked to discuss. (This latter topic must await additional analyses not conducted as part of the present study).

The dominant approach to the study of children's verbal communication focuses on spontaneous speech in naturalistic settings. Recently some investigators have turned to the study of discussions in groups, including the discussion of academic subject matter (Barnes & Todd, 1977; Webb, 1980, 1982, 1985). The reader should recall that the present study deals exclusively with group discussions where pupils were given a topic that was selected directly from the subject matter that was being studied in their classrooms, and that the group discussions were carefully limited to 15 minutes. Hence, the consistency with which the topic was selected as well as the duration of the discussion were controlled and uniform for all groups, not at all spontaneous. Therefore, topic consistency and discussion length could not be variables in this study. The cognitive strategies used here were constructed to serve the particular purposes of this study. These strategies, and their definitions, are as follows:

1. Explanation with evidence. The pupil had to provide a reason or explanation for the idea he expressed.

Example: "If there are a lot of people there are also a lot of cars and that's what makes pollution."

2. Unstructured idea. This category refers primarily to what is known as 'thinking out loud.' It is an association

expressed verbally that is not organized syntactically. Often it is comprised of short or disjointed sentences loosely linked together or largely disconnected.

Example: "Yeah. but that's not so good for agriculture, there's not enough... o.k....that's not considered...now we're talking about the New York area and Baltimore, and all that... the whole megalopolis... ."

3. Repetitions. The speaker repeats a statement of his/her own, or someone else's statement, almost verbatim.
4. Generalization. The speaker abstracts a principle or conclusion from his/her own or from another pupils' comments that is applicable to other instances, i.e. finds the common denominator underlying several phenomena.

Example: "I think the question is very relevant for our day... I'm not talking now about Jews in the communist-bloc countries... they too participate actively and some have lost their identity and don't consider themselves Jews, just like in Spain" (during the Middle Ages).

5. Concrete example.
     Example: "We can take Israel as an example.... ."
6. Takes a Stand. The speaker expresses a personal opinion on a given topic.

Example: "In my opinion we don't have to be
            influenced by their culture because every
            nation has its own culture."

7. <u>Presents a hypothesis or idea</u>. This refers only to an
idea that had not been expressed previously in the
discussion.

8. <u>Organizes ideas</u>. Someone tried to refocus the
discussion when it has gotten off track. Or, the speaker
attempts to relate what is being said at a given time with
something said earlier.

Example: "I think we should think again about the most
            important point, that... ."

9. <u>Repetition with expansion</u>. The pupil adds a new idea
or new connecting link to an idea that he/she is repeating
after it was made by a previous speaker.

CHAPTER 3: RESULTS

Academic Achievement

The achievement data were analysed in several different ways. First, class-level scores were used to ascertain if there were treatment effects above and beyond differences between classrooms (teachers). These analyses indicate that there is a disordinal relationship, i.e. no overlap, between the mean scores from the Group-Investigation classes and those from classes taught with the Whole-Class method. A Treatment x Class interaction revealed that some classes were better than others, but no class from the Whole-Class method was superior to any class in the Group-Investigation method (see Tables 23 and 24, pages 172 and 173).

It must be pointed out that, due to unfortunate events beyond our control that occurred in the school at the conclusion of this experiment, it was not possible to administer the posttest to one class in History and to two classes in Geography. The classes not tested did not differ in any way from the classes who responded to the posttest.

Pupils' individual scores were then used in a set of analyses of covariance where father's education was the covariate and pre- and post-test scores were the repeated measures. The means, SDs and F statistics from these analyses appear in Tables 2 and 3 (pages 67 and 69).

A third set of analyses had three treatment groups. The classes taught with the Whole-Class method were subdivided into those whose teachers had participated in the workshops about cooperative learning but who did not actually implement it in their classroom teaching, and those classes whose teachers neither participated in the workshops nor implemented cooperative learning methods. This subdivision was done to check for the possibility that the teachers' mere exposure to the workshops, without actually implementing cooperative learning, could have exerted a systematic effect on the children's academic achievement (Tables 4 and 5, pages 71 and 72).

The analysis of the individual-level scores yielded significant interaction effects for Treatment x Time on the low-level questions ($F=75.59$, $p<.001$), on the high-level questions of analysis and application ($F=63.22$, $p<.001$) and on the Total score ($F=94.44$, $p<.001$). Pupils from the Group-Investigation classes had consistently higher scores than their peers from the Whole-Class method.

Analysis of the Low-level and Total Score data also yielded a significant interaction effect for social-class/ethnicity indicating that the lower class/Middle-Eastern pupils generally progressed less from pretest to instructional methods. It is of interest to note that the Middle-Eastern pupils in the cooperative-learning classes managed to improve enough so that their scores were as high or higher than were those of the Western pupils in the Whole-Class method. But the students of Western

Table 2
Means, SDs and F Statistics of achievement scores in geography of Western and Middle-Eastern pupils in classes conducted with the Group-Investigation and Whole-Class instructional methods

Scale/ Time		G-I		W-C		F#
		W N = 127	ME N= 42	W N = 49	ME N = 19	
Low-level (0-41)						
pre	M	8.43	3.60	9.76	4.37	
	SD	6.13	3.54	8.59	3.73	75.59**
post	M	38.66	29.69	29.10	19.42	11.17**
	SD	5.86	9.12	7.95	9.85	
High-level (0-39)						
pre	M	8.96	3.81	8.69	5.58	
	SD	4.90	2.75	5.08	3.67	63.22**
post	M	27.67	22.74	20.41	14.84	
	SD	4.69	5.92	6.68	8.13	
Total (0-80)						
pre	M	17.33	7.36	18.45	9.95	
	SD	10.00	5.00	12.56	5.90	94.44**
						6.99**
post	M	66.29	52.52	49.51	34.26	
	SD	9.19	13.95	12.35	16.29	

*p < .01   # First F is interaction effect for Treatment x Time
**p < .001   #Second F is interaction effect for Ethnicity x Time

67

background improved more than their Middle-Eastern classmates. Consequently, the ethnic achievement gap was not narrowed <u>within</u> the cooperative-learning classes themselves. It was 'narrowed' only if one compares the scores of the Middle-Eastern/lower class students in the cooperative-learning classes to their ethnic peers in the Whole-Class method. Students from both ethnic groups clearly benefitted academically from being in the Group-Investigation classes, but the middle-class students retained their lead.

The means, SDs and F statistics of the History achievement data appear in Table 3 (see page 69). Again, findings for the Low-level, High-level and Total Scores indicated a distinctly superior effect of cooperative learning classes on the pupils' achievements when father's education is taken into consideration as a covariate. In these data, the Middle-Eastern pupils' scores were notably higher than those of the Western children in the Whole-Class method, but still significantly lower than those of their Western classmates, as indicated by the interaction effect for ethnicity/social class with time of measurement in each of the three measures.

Even though the cooperative learning experiences did not narrow the ethnic achievement gap, the fact that the Middle-Eastern students perform quite badly in the Whole-Class method should not be ignored.

As indicated above, a second set of analyses was performed with the classrooms conducted with the Whole-Class method subdivided into two groups: one whose teachers participated in the workshops, the other whose

Table 3
Means, SDs and F statistics of achievement scores in history of Western and Middle-Eastern pupils in classes conducted with the Group-Investigation and Whole-Class instructional methods

Scale/ Time		G-I		W-C		F#
		W N = 134	ME N = 47	W N = 60	ME N = 26	
Low-level (0-44)						
pre	M	11.22	7.62	12.98	7.12	
	SD	5.39	4.42	7.25	4.09	142.04**
						9.61*
post	M	38.87	31.38	26.57	17.42	
	SD	6.72	8.38	8.44	8.95	
High-level (0-36)						
pre	M	9.76	7.19	8.82	5.19	
	SD	5.72	4.56	6.14	4.91	46.31**
						7.23**
post	M	23.73	18.79	16.36	9.81	
	SD	5.92	7.60	7.40	6.32	
Total (0-80)						
pre	M	20.99	14.81	21.73	12.31	
	SD	9.20	7.20	10.53	7.05	129.26**
						11.79**
post	M	62.60	50.17	42.78	27.23	
	SD	10.85	14.44	14.40	13.73	

*p < .01   # First F is interaction effect for Treatment x Time
**p < .001   #Second F is interaction effect for Ethnicity x Time

teachers did not participate. Neither group implemented any of the cooperative-learning techniques in their classroom teaching. The primary purpose of these analyses was to ascertain if the teachers' participation in the workshops affected the students' academic perfomance in some systematic way without overt use of the cooperative learning procedures. Thus, our interest here is to compare the two subgroups of the Whole-Class method. These data appear in Tables 4 and 5 (see pages 71 and 72). On the Geography test, the no-participation - no implementation subgroup achieved the same or superior results on the Low-level questions for the Western pupils. These plus and minus signs always reflect a comparison across methods with members of the same ethnic group (see Table 6).

Table 6

Comparison of pupils' achievement scores in classes conducted with the Whole-Class method by teachers who did (P) and who did not (NP) participate in cooperative-learning workshops

| | Scale | WC-P | | WC-NP | |
		W	ME	W	ME
	L-L	-	+	+	-
Geography	H-L	0	+	0	-
	TS	-	+	+	-
	L-L	-	-	+	+
History	H-L	-	-	+	+
	TS	-	-	+	+

Table 4
Means, SDs and F statistics of achievement scores in history of pupils (N = 268) in two instructional methods and two ethnic groups, with teachers from different levels of training and implemetation

Scale		Workshops +G-I		Workshops +W-C		No Workshops +W-C		F#
		W	ME	W	ME	W	ME	
Low-level								
pre	M	11.22	7.61	11.16	6.94	16.14	7.44	
	SD	5.39	4.42	5.35	4.04	8.99	4.42	88.96***
								5.13*
post	M	38.87	31.38	22.08	13.47	34.32	24.89	
	SD	6.72	8.38	5.27	7.95	7.19	5.28	
High-level								
pre	M	9.76	7.19	7.59	4.24	11.00	7.00	
	SD	5.72	4.56	5.16	4.66	7.20	5.12	24.46***
								6.00**
post	M	23.73	18.79	13.95	8.29	20.64	12.67	
	SD	5.92	7.60	6.04	6.34	7.78	5.50	
Total								
pre	M	20.99	14.81	18.61	11.18	27.14	14.44	
	SD	9.20	7.20	8.79	6.43	11.28	8.03	76.19***
								7.73**
post	M	62.60	50.17	35.74	21.76	54.95	37.56	
	SD	10.85	14.44	9.51	12.98	13.35	8.28	

*p < .05   # First F is effect for interaction of Treatment x Time
**p < .01   Second F is effect for interaction Ethnicity x Time
***p < .001

Table 5
Means, SDs and F statistics of achievement scores in geography of pupils (N = 237) in two instructional methods and two ethnic groups, with teachers from different levels of training and implemetation

		Workshops +G-I		Workshops +W-C		No Workshops +W-C		F#
Scale		W	ME	W	ME	W	ME	
Low-level								
pre	M	8.43	3.60	8.36	4.50	10.89	4.22	
	SD	6.13	3.54	5.36	3.14	10.49	4.49	39.41***
								8.11**
post	M	38.66	29.69	25.45	21.90	32.07	16.67	
	SD	5.86	9.12	7.28	7.99	7.31	11.34	
High-level								
pre	M	8.96	3.81	6.86	3.80	10.19	7.56	
	SD	4.90	2.75	3.91	2.25	5.49	4.03	46.27***
								3.68*
post	M	27.67	22.74	21.05	18.70	19.89	10.56	
	SD	4.69	5.92	6.05	6.90	7.23	7.47	
Total								
pre	M	17.33	7.36	15.23	8.30	21.07	11.77	52.81***
	SD	10.00	5.00	8.60	4.62	14.69	6.87	6.92**
								3.50*
post	M	66.29	52.52	46.50	40.60	51.96	27.22	
	SD	9.19	13.95	11.88	12.03	12.40	18.12	

*p < .05   # First F is effect for interaction of Treatment x Time
**p < .01   Second F is effect for interaction Ethnicity x Time
***p < .001

Participation per se in the workshops did not yield systematic benefits for the pupils. The most systematic finding is that the Western students whose teachers did participate in the workshops but did not implement Group-Investigation, appear to have done worse than their ethnic peers whose teachers did not participate at all! Also, there is a distinct difference in these patterns as a function of subject matter. All students did worse in History with teachers who participated and better with the teachers who did not participate, although the reverse was true in Geography but for the Middle-Eastern students only. No simple hypothesis regarding a "Hawthorne" or "halo" effect can account for these findings.

Social Interaction

The second part of the findings in this study concerns the pupils' social interaction. Analyses of these data, as well as of those in the following section on the pupils' verbal behavior, concentrated on ethnic relations alongside our interest in the effects of the two teaching methods. The data regarding social and verbal interaction derive from two 15-minute discussions, one on a topic in Geography, the other on a topic in History. The discussions were conducted by mixed-ethnic groups with six pupils per group selected at random from each classroom. Data from the two discussions were combined and analyzed together. There was no theoretical basis for treating the data from the discussion of each subject separately, since the subject matter was not directly relevant to the primary concerns of this study. The same 6 pupils participated in both discussions, about Geography and History.

Correlations were calculated between all of the social-interaction categories to ascertain if they were redundant. We also wished to ascertain if it was justified to place several categories together into a scale assessing a similar topic. The Pearson correlations between the categories of social interaction appear in Table 7.

Table 7

Pearson correlations between categories of social behavior during 30 minutes of discussion in 6-person groups (N = 131)

Categories

	1	2	3	4	5	6	7	8
9	-.25	-.22	-.23	-.17	-.11	-.11	.28	.31
8	-.10	-.06	-.09	-.04	-.03	-.10	-.04	
7	-.50	-.35	-.43	-.27	-.27	-.14		
6	.36	.30	.37	.36	.48			
5	.41	.37	.32	.41				
4	.32	.29	.32					
3	.75	.57						
2	.56							

In light of the moderate to fairly large correlations between categories 1, 2, and 3, the data from these three categories

74

were added and analyzed as one measure of Cooperative Statements (Tables 8 and 9 see pages 76, 77 and 78), in addition to the analysis performed on the data in each category alone. The same was done with the data from categories 4, 5, and 6 that were combined into a scale called Conflicted Statements (Tables 10 and 11 see pages 79, 80 and 81) and analyzed together, in addition to the separate analysis of the data from each of these categories alone. The data for all of these categories were divided by the ethnic group of the speaker and of the person to whom the statement is addressed. The ethnic identity of the person to whom the statement is addressed appears at the top of the table, while the identity of the speaker appears in the row under the title of the teaching method.

In addition to the six categories of social interaction, the pupils' statements were also categorized as being directed at the entire group and not to any particular individual, and as being acts that were individualistic in nature, also not directed at anyone in particular or at the group as a whole. But these categories (7,8 and 9) did not correlate with one another so no composite score was calculated for all three as a scale. Each of the 10

Table 8

Means and SDs of cooperative acts directed at Western and at Middle-Eastern pupils during a 30-minute discussion in groups from classrooms taught with the Group-Investigation (N = 62)) or the Whole-Class (N = 69) method.

To Western

Category		G-I		W-C	
		W	ME	W	ME
1. Cooperation	M	5.52	4.48	7.27	3.91
on task	SD	5.16	4.53	6.99	4.15
2. Social	M	0.67	1.28	1.49	0.72
Cooperation	SD	0.82	1.33	1.84	1.20
3. Listening to	M	15.76	13.28	19.81	12.84
respond	SD	10.25	8.58	11.94	9.36
Total					
Cooperative	M	21.94	19.03	28.57	17.47
Interaction	SD	14.91	12.49	18.86	12.30

Table 8 (continued)

To Middle-Eastern

Category		G-I		W-C	
		W	ME	W	ME
1. Cooperation	M	4.45	2.59	3.00	0.88
on task	SD	4.05	3.04	3.16	1.79
2. Social	M	1.33	0.41	1.08	0.34
Cooperation	SD	1.59	0.73	2.05	0.87
3. Listening to	M	13.12	7.69	9.46	4.19
respond	SD	7.15	5.74	8.34	5.24
Total					
Cooperative	M	18.91	10.69	13.54	5.41
Interaction	SD	10.21	8.61	11.86	7.09

Table 9

F-Statistics and p values for cooperative acts

Category	To Western		To Middle-Eastern	
	Source	F	Source	F
1. Cooperation on task	Main effect for ethnic group	5.68*	1. Method	8.27**
			Ethnic group	13.37***
2. Social cooperation	Interaction effect	8.26*	2. Ethnic group	10.39**
3. Listening to respond	Main-effect for ethnic group	7.31**	3. Method	9.02**
			Ethnic group	20.01***
Total Cooperation	Main effect for ethnic group	7.44***	Method	9.79**
			Ethnic group	22.99***

*p < .05

**p < .01

***p < .001

78

Table 10

Means and SDs of non-cooperative acts directed at Western and at Middle-Eastern pupils during a 30-minute discussion in groups from classrooms taught with the Group-Investigation or Whole-Class method.

To Western

Category		G-I		W-C	
		W	ME	W	ME
4. Competition	M	0.82	0.10	0.76	0.28
on task	SD	3.66	0.41	1.36	0.58
5. Critical	M	1.00	0.52	2.78	1.31
Comments	SD	1.84	1.21	4.26	2.10
6. Oppostion	M	1.39	1.83	2.49	1.19
	SD	1.62	3.96	2.74	1.94
Total					
Conflicted	M	3.21	2.45	6.03	2.78
Interaction	SD	4.82	4.45	6.87	3.32

Table 10 (continued)

To Middle-Eastern

| | | G-I | | W-C | |
| | | W | ME | W | ME |
Category					
4. Competition	M	0.58	0.21	0.41	0.16
	SD	1.84	0.77	0.83	0.45
5. Critical	M	0.85	0.38	1.38	0.22
Comments	SD	1.28	0.82	2.03	0.55
6. Opposition	M	1.79	1.59	1.27	0.44
	SD	2.30	2.71	1.45	1.16
Total					
Conflicted	M	3.21	2.17	3.05	0.81
Interaction	SD	4.30	3.77	2.92	1.64

Table 11

F-Statistics and p values for non-cooperative behavior data

	To Western		To Middle-Eastern	
Category	Source	F	Source	F
4. Competition	-	-	-	-
5. Critical Comments	Main effect for method	7.86**	Ethnic group	12.52***
	Main effect for ethnic group	4.51*		
6. Opposition	-	-	Method	5.56**
Total	Method	3.42*		
	Ethnic Group	5.32**	Ethnic Group	8.39**

*p < .05

**p < .01

***p < .001

81

categories, and the total scores of each scale of cooperative, non-cooperative, individualistic and group-oriented statements, was analyzed by a 2-way analysis of variance, with instructional methods (2) and ethnic group (2) as factors. Data from statements addressed to Western pupils and to Middle-Eastern pupils were analyzed separately.

We will focus primarily on the results from the analyses of the Total scores for each of the two scales, i.e. cooperative acts (Tables 8,9), and non-cooperative acts (Tables 10,11) and on the results for the four measures of individual and group-oriented statements (Tables 12, 13 see pages 83 and 84).

Western pupils received more cooperative statements from other Westerners than from Middle-Eastern pupils regardless of instructional method. (Main effect for ethnic group for Total number of cooperative statements made to Western students: $F = 7.44$, $p < .01$). The number of such statements to Western pupils by Middle-Eastern pupils was very similar in groups from both instructional methods (19.03 in Group-Investigation classes, 17.47 in the Whole-Class method).

A very different picture emerged in the data about the cooperative statements made to pupils of Middle-Eastern background in the discussion groups. Those who had studied in the Group-Investigation classes received more cooperative statements than their ethnic peers from the Whole-Class method (Main-effect for method: $F = 9.79$, $p < .01$). Western pupils in the discussion groups from both teaching methods made many more cooperative statements

82

Table 12

Group-oriented and Individualistic acts during group discussions

7. Individualistic acts related to task	M	4.58	5.28	9.30	10.44
	SD	3.67	3.94	7.13	6.98
8. Individualistic acts not related to task	M	1.15	3.28	4.16	4.66
	SD	1.60	12.89	3.98	4.66
9. Confused acts	M	5.67	6.52	6.32	11.28
	SD	5.74	4.67	6.51	6.49
10. Cooperative Statements addressed to entire group	M	19.03	16.55	18.32	9.91
	SD	9.10	10.71	6.63	8.72

Table 13

F statistics and p values for group-oriented and individualistic behavior

Category	Source of Effects	F	p
7.	Main effect for method	22.51	<.001
8.	Main effect for method	3.51	<.06
9.	Main effect for method	6.10	<.01
	Main effect for ethnic group	8.36	<.01
To entire	Main effect for method	5.11	<.05
group	Main effect for ethnic group	13.27	<.001

to the Middle-Eastern students in these groups than were made by Middle-Easterners to one another (main effect for ethnic group: $F = 22.99$, $p < .001$). Nonethless, Middle-Eastern pupils from the Group-Investigation classes were addressed cooperatively by their ethnic peers twice as frequently as they were when coming from classes taught by the Whole-Class method (Middle-Eastern to Middle-Eastern in Group-Investigation class = Mean of 10.69; Middle Eastern to Middle-Eastern in Whole-Class method = Mean of 5.41). The Middle-Eastern pupils in the Whole-Class method again appeared to be the group that was much worse off than all the other groups in this study, in terms of receiving support from their classmates.

Of particular interest is the finding that Western and Middle-Eastern pupils from the Group-Investigation classrooms made almost the same number of cooperative statements to members of the other ethnic group (Middle-Eastern to Western = 19.03; Western to Middle-Eastern = 18.91). However, this reciprocity in inter-ethnic support found among pupils from the Group-Investigation method was not found among pupils from the Whole-Class method (Middle-Eastern to Western = 17.47; Western to Middle-Eastern = 13.54).

Another contrast that deserves attention is the number of cooperative statements made by students from the same teaching method. In the discussion groups selected from the Group-Investigation method, Western pupils were addressed cooperatively at an equal rate by pupils from their own as well as from the Middle-Eastern group (Western to Western = 21.94; Middle-Eastern to Western

18.91). Yet, Middle-Eastern pupils addressed far fewer cooperative statements to other members of their own ethnic group than they did to the Westerners in their discussion groups (Middle-Eastern to Western = 19.03; Middle-Eastern to Middle-Eastern = 10.69). We should recall that the Western pupils made almost as many cooperative statements to Middle Easterners (18.91) as they did to their own ethnic peers (21.94) in groups from the Group-Investigation classes.

In the groups from the Whole-Class method, the pre-eminent status of the Western pupils is even more evident. Here there is no symmetry in the number of statements made by Westerners to pupils from their own and from the Middle-Eastern group (Western to Western = 28.57; Western to Middle-Eastern = 13.54), with the latter receiving about one-third the number of cooperative statements as did the Western pupils (more than one standard deviation). The same finding emerged in respect to the statements made by Middle-Eastern pupils from the Whole-Class method: They addressed three times as many cooperative statements to Western pupils in their discussion groups as they did to their Middle-Eastern peers (Middle-Eastern to Western = 17.47; Middle-Eastern to Middle-Eastern = 5.41).

The overall number of competitive and critical statements expressed in the discussion groups was not very large, and there were few differences on these measures between the groups from the two teaching methods (Tables 10 and 11). The most salient finding indicates that there were more conflicted statements addressed to the Western pupils in the groups from the

Whole-Class method than in those from the Group-Investigation classes (Table 11: $F = 3.42$, $p < .05$). Western pupils were twice as critical toward each other in Whole-Class than in Group-Investigation classes, while the amount of competitive and critical statements addressed by Middle-Eastern to Western students in their groups remained unchanged.

Tables 12 and 13 present the data about statements not addressed to specific persons in the group but to the group as a whole, or statements made without clear reference to anyone and, hence, were categorized as individualistic remarks. There was also a category of statements that reflected confusion. All of these categories revealed that more such statements were made in the groups from the Whole-Class than from the Group-Investigation classes. Again, the number of cooperative statements addressed to the group as a whole by pupils from both ethnic groups was almost identical in the groups from the Group-Investigation classes, while there was a large gap favoring the Western students in the Whole-Class method. Obviously the pupils from the Whole-Class method were more individually oriented than their peers from the Group-Investigation classes and were less able to work as part of a group. The pupils from the Whole-Class method expressed far more confused statements in their groups than their ethnic peers who had studied in the Group-Investigation classes.

Verbal Behavior

Three measures of verbal behavior were employed in this study: Frequency of speech, comprised of the number of words per turn of speech spoken by pupils in the discussion groups, and the number of times each pupil spoke (data in Tables 16 and 17; see page 90); focused interactions, consisting of 6 categories of types of speech (data in Tables 18 and 19; see pages 91 and 92); cognitive strategies, consisting of 9 strategies that appeared in the pupils' speech (data in Tables 20 and 21; see pages 94 and 95). Pearson correlations between the 6 categories of focused interactions appear in Table 14, and between the 9 categories of cognitive strategies in Table 15. These correlations reveal that most of the categories are moderately related, although some do over-lap more extensively, particularly in the six categories of focused interactions. All in all they appear to be evaluating different aspects of the same phenomena, though categories 2 and 6 of the focused interactions can be viewed as redundant.

Table 14

Pearson correlations between categories of focused interactions in pupils' verbal behavior (N = 131)

	1	2	3	4	5
6	.22	.85	.11	.11	.84
5	.27	.76	.29	.01	
4	.18	.14	.40		
3	.41	.19			
2	.33				

Table 15

Pearson correlations between different cognitive strategies in pupils' verbal behavior

	1	2	3	4	5	6	7	8
9	.39	.27	.55	.09	.37	.41	.34	.21
8	-.06	.81	.13	.09	.79	.10	.16	
7	.36	.09	.35	.26	.17	.19		
6	.45	.09	.56	.04	.16			
5	.16	.15	.15	.18				
4	.16	.15	.15					
3	.38	.09						
2	-.02							

Analysis of the number of words spoken revealed a main effect for teaching method and for ethnic group (Tables 16 and 17). Pupils in the discussion groups from the Group-Investigation classes spoke more words per turn of speech than did pupils from the Whole-Class method (F = 4.16, p < .05). Predictably, the pupils from Western ethnic background said more words than pupils from Middle-Eastern background, in groups from both instructional methods (F = 4.05, p < .05). The cooperative learning method increased the number of words that pupils used in a given span of time (30 minutes of discussion allotted to each group). However, it did not decrease the size of the discrepancy between children from the two ethnic groups in terms of the mean number of words they used per turn of speech in the group discussions.

Table 16
Means and SDs of frequency of Western and Middle-Eastern pupils' speech in groups from classes conducted with the Group-Investigation and Whole-Class instructional methods during a 30-minute discussion.

Measure		G-I		W-C	
		W	ME	W	ME
Number of words	M	16.73	13.93	13.92	11.75
spoken per turn	SD	12.04	8.28	9.33	9.20
Number of turns	M	38.18	35.54	44.73	25.88
taken to speak	SD	17.19	19.87	20.31	19.12

Table 17
F-statistics and p values of data from frequency of pupils' speech

Measure	Source of effect	F	p
Number of words	Main effect for method	4.16	<.05
	Main effect for ethnic group	4.05	<.05
Number of turns	Interaction effect	5.75	<.01

90

Table 18

Means and SDs of Western and Middle-Eastern pupils' verbal behavior in 6 categories of focused interactions in groups from classes conducted with Group-Investigation and Whole-Class methods

		G-I		W-C	
Category		W	ME	W	ME
1. Requests	M	2.45	1.72	2.97	1.77
clarification	SD	3.89	1.73	2.41	2.36
2. Gives	M	2.94	0.83	2.59	1.55
clarification	SD	5.54	0.97	2.77	2.73
3. Agreement	M	2.09	1.07	2.11	1.03
	SD	2.52	1.62	2.31	1.47
4. Disagreement	M	3.91	2.07	2.35	1.71
	SD	10.30	2.31	2.26	2.34
5. Directive	M	6.85	3.24	7.51	3.13
	SD	16.04	2.99	7.80	3.05
6. Interruptions	M	2.48	2.28	4.08	3.26
	SD	2.36	2.20	5.66	4.10

Table 19
F-statistics for data on verbal behavior

Category	Source of Effect	F	p
1	Main effect for ethnic group	4.10	<.05
2	Main effect for ethnic group	6.53	<.01
3	Main effect for ethnic group	8.42	<.01
4	No effects	-	< -
5	Main effect for ethnic group	5.98	<.01
6	Main effect for method	3.17	<.07

The interaction effect (F = 5.75, p < .01) obtained from the analysis of the number of turns taken during the discussions means that the Western pupils took more turns to speak in groups from the Whole-Class method, but fewer turns in the groups from the Group-Investigation classes. The opposite was true for the Middle-Eastern pupils who took fewer turns in the groups from the Whole-Class method and more turns in the groups from the Group-Investigation method (Tables 16 and 17). The net result of this finding is that there is a very large discrepancy in number of turns of speech taken by Western and by Middle-Eastern Jewish children who studied in the Whole-Class method, while this discrepancy virtually does not exist in the groups who studied in the Group-Investigation classrooms.

Data obtained from the analyses of the discussions with the categories of 'focused interaction' yielded almost no differences as a function of teaching method except for category 6, 'interruptions,' where the groups consisting of pupils from the Group-Investigation classes were found to interrupt each other less than in the groups from the Whole-Class method. All of the other findings reflect differences between the ethnic groups regardless of teaching method (Categories 1, 2, 3 and 5), with the Western pupils displaying these categories in their speech more frequently than the Middle-Eastern pupils (Tables 18 and 19).

The final set of data about the pupils' verbal behavior refers to the frequency with which the pupils employed various cognitive strategies in their speech (Tables 20 and 21). Two-way Analyses of Variance, with teaching methods (2) and ethnic groups (2) as factors, yielded significant effects for teaching method in only two out of the nine categories, namely category 6 (takes a stand) and 8 (organizes ideas). In both cases, pupils from the Group-Investigation classes used these categories more frequently in their speech than the pupils from the Whole-Class method.

Table 20
Means and SDs of Western and Middle-Eastern pupils' verbal behavior in nine strategies of cognitive functioning in groups from classes conducted with Group-Investigation and Whole-Class methods.

| | | G-I | | W-C | |
Strategy		W	ME	W	ME
1. Explanation with	M	2.42	2.07	2.43	1.03
evidence	SD	1.68	1.79	2.41	1.08
2. Unstructured	M	1.76	.45	1.00	.58
idea	SD	6.94	.63	1.37	.96
3. Repetitions	M	5.33	5.03	7.32	3.87
	SD	3.82	3.11	5.45	3.89
4. Generalization	M	.18	.03	.35	.10
	SD	.53	.19	.79	.30
5. Concrete	M	5.94	2.79	3.24	1.45
examples	SD	15.75	3.00	3.47	1.31
6. Takes a stand	M	10.45	8.00	8.32	4.10
	SD	9.33	5.68	7.91	5.02
7. Presents a	M	2.88	2.17	3.70	1.77
hypothesis	SD	2.46	2.28	2.79	1.76
8. Organizes	M	1.64	.76	.54	.52
ideas	SD	3.90	1 .38	.93	.89
9. Repetition with	M	1.72	.62	2.14	.74
expansion	SD	1.46	.90	1.99	1.39
TOTAL	M	32.30	21.93	29.05	14.16
	SD	30.93	12.76	17.63	11.60

Table 21

F-statistics for nine categories of cognitive strategies in pupils' verbal behavior.

Category	Source of Effect	F	p
1	Main effect for ethnic group	7.79	<.01
2	No effects	-	-
3	Main effect for ethnic group	6.86	<.01
4	Main effect for ethnic group	4.81	<.05
5	No effects	-	-
6	Main effect for method	5.31	<.05
	Main effect for ethnic group	6.94	<.01
7	Main effect for ethnic group	10.32	<.01
8	Main effect for method	3.38	<.06
9	Main effect for ethnic group	21.75	<.001
Total	Main effect for ethnic group	13.09	<.001

A close examination of the mean scores recorded for these categories, particularly the Total scores for all nine categories, suggested that the two-way analysis was masking important differences between pupils who had studied in the Group-Investigation and Whole-Class methods. Consequently, we decided to employ a one-way Analysis of Variance that compared the mean scores of all four groups, Western and Middle-Eastern pupils from the Group-Investigation classes, and Western and Middle-

95

Eastern pupils from the Whole-Class method. This analysis yielded an F of 5.43 ($p < .01$) for the Total mean scores on the cognitive strategies. The scores derived from the contrasts calculated between each pair of mean scores revealed that the scores of the Middle-Eastern pupils in the two teaching methods differed significantly, and the Middle-Eastern pupils from the Group-Investigation classes obtained higher scores on the total number of cognitive strategies than did the Middle-Eastern pupils from the Whole-Class method ($t = 2.54$, $p < .01$). Indeed, the difference of 7.7 between the two means is more than half of the standard deviation of these means. The gap in scores between the Western and Middle-Eastern pupils in the Group-Investigation classes is somewhat smaller than the gap between those two groups from the Whole-Class method. This same pattern was found for category 1 (explanation with evidence) ($t = 2.22$, $p < .05$), category 5 (concrete examples) ($t = 2.19$, $p < .05$) and category 6 (takes a stand) ($t = 2.92$, $p < .01$). In all three instances the scores of the Middle-Eastern pupils from the two teaching methods differed significantly, with pupils from the Group-Investigation classes getting the higher scores. In category 3 (repetitions) the Western pupils from the Whole-Class method received higher scores than the Western pupils from the Group-Investigation classes ($t = 1.97$, $p < .05$).

Relationship between Pupil Behavior in the Discussions and their Academic Achievement

The last set of data to be presented here are the results of a series of regression analyses conducted with the scores obtained on the various measures of the pupils' behavior in the discussion groups. These regression analyses were used to determine the relationship between the pupils' behavior during the discussion sessions and their scores on the tests of academic achievement (pre-test/post-test difference scores adjusted for father's education). In particular we wished to learn if the measures of group interaction yielded information that was related to the pupils' achievement on formal tests, and to what extent this relationship obtained for each of the two levels of questions that appeared on the tests, i.e. questions that required low-level information or questions that required a higher level of intellectual performance, such as analysis and application of information to new situations. The findings from these analyses appear in Table 22 (see page 99). The independent variables used to predict the pupils' achievement scores in History and Geography included their scores on the scales of Cooperation and Conflict, the number of words and turns of speech, scores on the scale of focused interactions and on the total frequency of cognitive strategies. All of the analyses, for low and high level questions on the test of Geography, and on the low and high level History tests, yielded statistically significant findings, although the percentage of the variance explained in each case was modest: 21% of the variance in the scores from the low-level questions on the post test in History (F=3.56, p<.001) was explained by all of the independent variables. Of this, 6% was accounted for by fathers' education and 15% by the social and verbal process variables. 15% of the variance in the high-level questions on the post-test in History were explained by the independent variables (F=2.36, p<.05). On these questions, fathers' education explained 5% of the variance and the process variables accounted for 8%. On the low-level questions in Geography of the 22% of the variance explained by the independent variables (F=3.80, p<.002), 17% were accounted for by fathers' education and 5% by the process variables. Of the 19% of the variance explained in the high-level questions on the post-test in Geography (F = 3.24, p < .001), 14% were accounted for by fathers' education and 5% by the social and verbal process variables. All of the above findings were statistically significant.

It should be recalled that, even though some of the process measures were correlated to a moderate degree (see Table 25, page 175), they were all derived from the same group discussions. The achievement scores, on the other hand, were obtained from written tests administered several weeks after the discussion sessions were completed. Obviously, the process-product relationship should be studied during the actual sessions where the product is reached. Even with the attenuation of the process-product relationship that occurred in this study, which is typical of classrooms where achievement is measured after the completion of the process, a noteworthy portion of the variance in the product scores (achievement) was explained by the social and verbal process scores.

Table 22

Stepwise multiple regresson analyses with father's education and pupils' behavior in discussions as independent variables, and post-test achievement scores as dependent variables (N=130).

Independent Variables	Achievement Scale	R	R Change	F
History				
Fathers' education		.06		2.92*
Pupils' social and verbal behavior	Low-Level	.21	.15	3.56**
Fathers' education		.07		2.95*
Pupils' behavior	High-Level	.15	.08	2.36*
Geography				
Fathers' education		.17		8.61**
Pupils' behavior	Low Level	.22	.05	3.80**
Fathers' education		.14		7.15**
Pupil's behavior	High-Level	.19	.05	3.24**

* $p < .05$ ** $p < .001$

99

CHAPTER 4: DISCUSSION

The two instructional methods that constituted the independent variable in this study produced a wide range of differential effects on the pupils' academic achievement in History and Geography, on their social interaction and on their verbal behavior. Clearly, all these dimensions of children's behavior are significantly affected by their school experience, a fact frequently ignored by investigators from a variety of disciplines who are concerned with children's development and schooling. The effects found in this study were largely as predicted, but there were many unanticipated findings as well. Some results can be considered to be most unusual by comparison with the data reported in the research available thus far on the effects of cooperative learning (Slavin, Sharan, Kagan et al, 1985).

A broad overview of most of the findings obtained in this experiment can be gained by comparing several graphs, side by side, that summarize the data from the different measures (Figures 1-7). This way of viewing the findings highlights several important conclusions that may not be immediately evident from reading the statistical tables. The first conclusion is that, in terms of all the measures used in this study, the Whole-Class , traditional form of instruction is least beneficial for lower-class, Middle-

Eastern children in multiethnic classrooms. This group got 'the short end of the stick' in the Whole-Class method on every measure used here, in the domains of academic achievement, social interaction and verbal-intellectual behavior. Secondly, both the lower-class, Middle-Eastern pupils and the middle-class, Western pupils gained considerably from participating in the cooperative-learning classes. In several important instances (Figures 2, 3 and 6) the gap in academic and verbal-intellectual performance between pupils from the Western and from the Middle-Eastern group was distinctly narrowed or even closed when they studied in the classes taught with the Group-Investigation method, without this change involving any loss of progress on the part of Western pupils.

Figure 1: Mean Difference Scores on Achievement Test in Geography of Western and Middle-Eastern Pupils from the Group-Investigation and Whole-Class Methods.

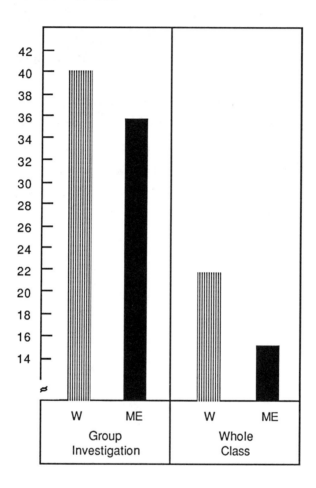

Figure 2: Mean Difference Scores on Achievement Test in History of Western and Middle-Eastern Pupils from the Group-Investigation and Whole-Class Methods.

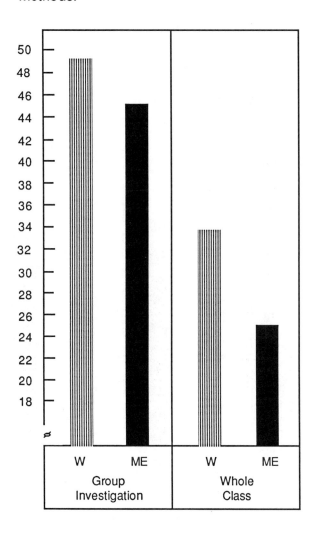

Figure 3: Mean Number of Cooperative Statements Addressed to Western and to Middle-Eastern Pupils from Group-Investigation and Whole-Class Methods by Western and Middle-Eastern Pupils in the Discussion Groups.

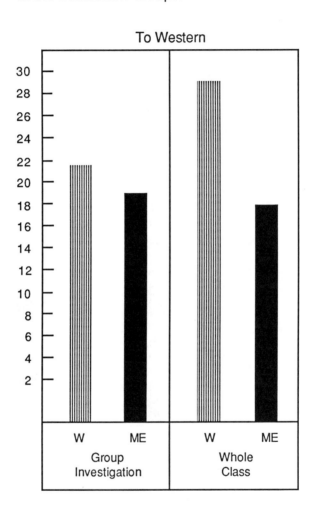

Figure 3 (continued)

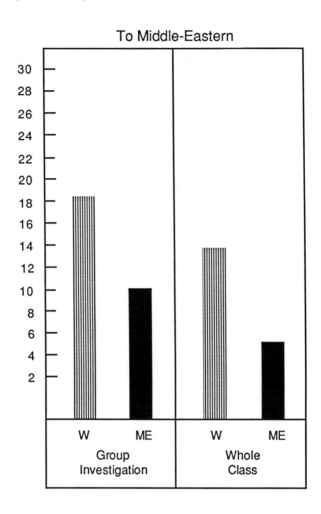

To Middle-Eastern

Figure 4: Mean Number of Non-Cooperative Statements Addressed to Western and Middle-Eastern Pupils from the Group-Investigation and Whole-Class Methods by Western and Middle-Eastern Pupils in the Discussion Groups.

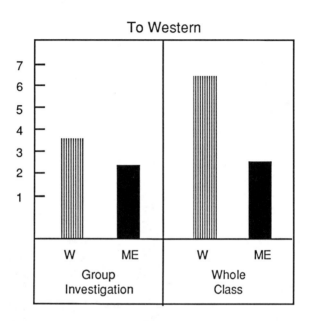

Figure 4 (continued)

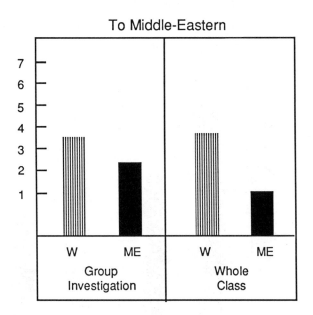

To Middle-Eastern

Figure 5: Mean Number of Words Per Turn Spoken by Western and Middle-Eastern Pupils from Group-Investigation and Whole-Class Methods During the Group Discussion.

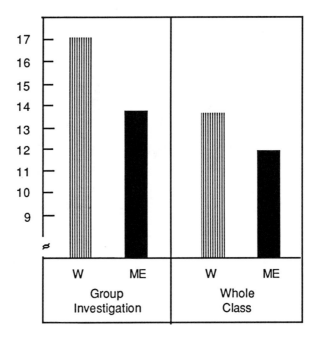

Figure 6: Mean Number of Turns Taken by Western and Middle-Eastern Pupils from Group-Investigation and Whole-Class Methods During the Group Discussion.

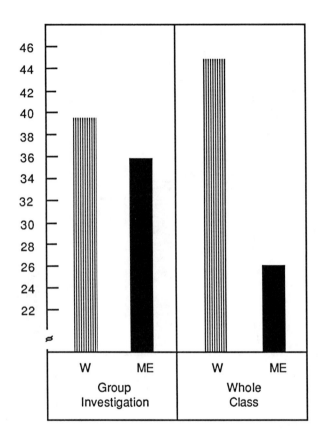

Figure7: Mean Number of Cognitive Strategies Appearing
in the Speech of Western and Middle-Eastern
Pupils from Group-Investigation and Whole-Class
Methods During the Group Discussion

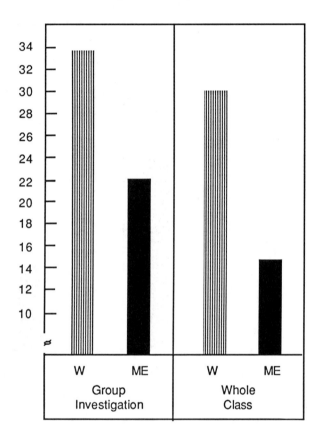

In their social and verbal interaction, both ethnic groups functioned more similarly in the Group-Investigation classes than they did in the traditional Whole-Class method where the gap between them was much more marked. On many measures the Group-Investigation classes promoted relatively symmetrical relations and participation between members of the two ethnic groups while there was a large gap in their behavior in the classes taught with the Whole-Class method. Clearly, the Middle-Eastern pupils emerged as the primary benefactors from having studied in the Group-Investigation classes, socially and verbally, without detracting from the benefits derived by the Western pupils as well. There can be little doubt, on the basis of these findings, that the multiethnic classroom conducted with the traditional Whole-Class method leaves the lower-class, Middle-Eastern children at a great disadvantage. There were also findings, not presented in graphic form, to the effect that the pupils from the Group-Investigation classes displayed more group-oriented behavior and much less individualistic and confused behavior during the group discussions than their peers from the Whole-Class classes.

We will discuss first the meaning of the results regarding the pupils' academic achievement. Following that, a special section will be devoted to the discussion of the findings about the pupils' social and verbal behavior in the discussion groups. Finally, we will discuss the results of the "process-product" analysis, i.e. the relationship between the data gathered in the discussions and the pupils' scores on the achievement tests.

111

Academic Achievement

Results obtained here about the pupils' academic achievement as a function of their participation in one of two different instructional methods yielded particularly large differences, indicating a distinctly superior effect of the Group-Investigation method in both History and Geography. This finding emerged on questions that required answers with simple information and comprehension, as well as on questions that could be answered only by applying knowledge to new problems, synthesizing different ideas, making inferences and reaching conclusions. Perusal of the research on pupils' academic achievement in cooperative learning classrooms suggests that the size of the differences reported here between the Group-Investigation and the Whole-Class methods are among the largest found thus far. Reviews of achievement studies concentrated on the differences found between pupils who studied in cooperative learning classrooms and the traditional 'frontal teaching' classes called the Whole-Class instruction in this report (Johnson, Maruyama, Johnson, Nelson and Skon, 1981; Slavin, 1980, 1983; Sharan, 1980; 1984). All of these reviews concluded that cooperative learning methods more often than not yielded superior academic outcomes for pupils from different ethnic groups and/or social classes who studied together in the same classroom. The present study shows that the extent of these outcomes can be considerable, and not just statistically significant.

Several steps were taken to reduce the possibility that the findings obtained here about academic achievement would be caused by extraneous factors. The distribution of the pupils' scores on each question was examined to determine if a large number of pupils failed the item, i.e. received very low scores, or if they systematically ignored certain questions, i.e. no response. This scrutiny of the scores on each item led to the decision to discard the data obtained with two of the items on the History achievement test that were not answered by a large number of pupils from the classrooms conducted with the Whole-Class method. Also, as another precaution against bias from extraneous factors, the achievement data were analyzed using the educational level of the pupils' fathers as a co-variate. This was done to correct for any bias introduced by the fact that pupils from the different ethnic groups/social classes were not distributed with complete symmetry in the two instructional methods despite the fact that the representation of these groups in the classrooms conducted with each of the two methods was carefully controlled by the school authorities.

Particularly reassuring in regard to the reliability of the achievement tests, is the fact that the pretest mean scores (and their standard deviations) for each ethnic group in the Group-Investigation compared to the Whole-Class method, were quite similar, and, in some instances, close to identical. As a result of these precuations, we are fairly confident that the achievement scores reported here are a close reflection of the effects on the pupils' learning generated by the teaching methods.

113

What can explain why the achievement results in this study are so much more salient than in many earlier studies (compare Sharan, 1984, chapter 2)? First and foremost we can attribute this result to the effectiveness with which the cooperative learning method used here, Group-Investigation, was implemented in this study compared to other experiments. Relatively superior implementation was made possible by the conditions of the research grant to the senior author that allowed for a year's time to train the teachers and prepare the curricular materials. The experiment proper was begun only during the second year. Teachers of the Group-Investigation method had an opportunity to acquire confidence in the application of their newly-acquired skills. In earlier experiments the constraints of the budget required that the teachers be trained and carry out the experimental procedures all during the course of a single academic year (Sharan, 1984). Of course this meant that the teachers of the cooperative learning classes, who had a few months' experience with the new techniques, were being compared to teachers who had many years of practice with the Whole-Class method, in terms of their effects on their pupils' learning. The present study is the only one known to these authors that was conducted with teachers who had some experience with cooperative learning in the year prior to the one where measures were taken of their pupils' progress and behavior. Even with these improved conditions relative to earlier research, the teachers in this study who taught with the Group-Investigation method were still far from accomplished practitioners of this approach, by comparison to the experience they had with traditional Whole-Class teaching. This striking imbalance in teacher proficiency with the cooperative learning versus the Whole-Class method remains a serious hinderance to the proper assessment of the effects of cooperative learning on pupils. Furthermore, the pupils' academic achievement in the study was assessed only on their knowledge about the third out of three curricular units that were taught with the Group-Investigation Method. This arrangement allowed the <u>pupils</u> to acquire skill in the group procedures before their academic performance was evaluated.

Returning once more to the graphs, we observe that the achievement gap between the two ethnic groups remained unchanged in the History classes in both teaching methods, even though the level of achievement in the two methods differed considerably. Of course, it is decidedly not the same to have a gap of 6.25 points between scores of 41.61 and 35.36, as occurred in the Group-Investigation classes, compared to a gap between the ethnic groups of 6.13 points between scores of 21.05 and 14.92 in the Whole-Class method. The former situation is distinctly superior in quality to the latter one and indicates an altogether different kind of relationship between the two groups. There is a great deal of difference in a comparison between two groups of high level performers versus a comparison between two groups of low level performers. But beyond this difference it should be noted that the gap in scores between the two groups in the Geography classes was markedly smaller (3.80) in the Group-Investigation classes than it was in the classes taught with the Whole-Class method (7.65).

It should be emphasized that the Western pupils attending the school where this experiment took place came from families with an unusually high percentage of professional parents or of parents with academic careers, while the pupils from lower-class, Middle-Eastern homes were 'bused' to the school from particularly poor neighborhoods where most of the parents had not completed grade school. This gap in educational, and not only in economic, background of the two ethnic groups as they were represented in this study may be larger than the educational gap between different ethnic groups found in other studies. In light of the truly vast differences in the educational background of the pupils' parents (Table 1), with 100 fathers of pupils from the Western group versus 7 fathers of pupils from Middle-Eastern background in the Group-Investigation classes who attended some institution of higher learning, it is unreasonable to anticipate that the academic achievement gap between the two groups could possibly be closed in one educational experiment (or even over the course of years). Yet findings reported here indicate significant benefits in learning for the pupils of Middle-Eastern background in the classes taught with the Group-Investigation method. There are also suggestions in the data from these classrooms of more symmetrical patterns of social interaction and verbal expression between pupils from the two ethnic groups.

All of these results point to the potential progress that can be made in fostering pupil achievement by changing

116

the basic approach to instruction in the classroom, albeit without eliminating the inter-ethnic gap, even when the educational background of the different ethnic groups is as great as occurred in this study. Other experiments with cooperative instructional methods in the multi-ethnic classrooms also reported improved academic achievement for lower-class or minority group pupils, without claiming to eradicate the academic gap between different social groups (Eshel and Klein, 1984; Johnson, Maruyama, Johnson, Nelson and Skon, 1981; Kagan, Zahn, et al, 1985; Sharan and Rich, 1984; Slavin, 1983;).

Cooperative Learning, Achievement and Motivation

When the Group-Investigation method is implemented with a reasonable degree of competence, pupils display a relatively high level of motivation and involvement in their learning activities. They initiate plans for gathering and synthesizing information from a variety of sources, they discuss the topic with one another, and the subject occupies their interest and attention, even arouses enthusiasm. Heightened involvement, interest and attention contribute greatly to the students' level of achievement, as has been demonstrated often (DeCharms, 1977), and not only the bare fact of spending more 'time-on task.'

Observation of most lessons conducted in the traditional Whole-Class format, where the flow of communication is primarily from the teacher to the students, will reveal little if any enthusiasm, and boredom is rampant.

(It should be noted that the vast majority of classes in Israel's secondary schools are still taught in this fashion). Even if the teacher is doing what appears to other adults as a yeoman's job, the students often remain bored if for no other reason that they are seated most of the time and follow the same routine endlessly, day after day. They have little opportunity for initiative, self expression or direct interaction with peers, and they exercise almost no control over their work in school (Ames and Ames, 1985).

The effects of motivation on cooperative learning outcomes has been studied primarily through the use of various reward systems, such as group or individual rewards, intergroup competition, etc. But the study of teaching effects on achievement as a result of various reward strategies actually teaches us more about the rewards than it does about teaching, and we learn little about the substance of motivation. Slavin is quite accurate when he writes that "incentive structure is used to refer to the means of motivating students to perform learning tasks" (Slavin, 1983, 1). We learn about the MEANS that were used to motivate students and how effective those particular means proved to be. However, we claim that very little has been learned about how the teaching methods themselves attract students and hold their interest.

Teachers in Israel have voiced objection to rewarding students for learning, even by the use of class newspapers that publish the names of pupils who excelled. That is one reason why the present authors have not conducted experiments using various tangible reward systems. But the more decisive reason is that the Group-Investigation approach to instruction is based on theoretical principles that emphasize the importance of 'intrinsic motivation,' of arousing students' involvement by structuring the learning situation to maximize their initiative and responsibility for their learning, both individually and collectively. In a recent study by the first author and a colleague, pupils who had spent the previous year in cooperative learning classes were given the option of remaining in their classrooms to continue their work on school tasks or go outside and play during recess. This procedure was repeated four times during the course of the year. Many more pupils from the cooperative learning classes elected to remain inside and not go out to the school yard, compared to pupils from the traditionally taught classes (Sharan and Shaulov, 1986). This behavioral, non-intrusive measure of pupil motivation to pursue their studies indicates that the cooperative learning approach to instruction does in fact generate more willingness to persevere at school tasks than the Whole-Class approach, without the use of any extrinsic reward system. Indeed, these pupils were actually asked to sacrifice an activity that most children perceive to be a highlight of their school day. We were surprised that anyone at all would be prepared to stay indoors and get nothing in return except the opportunity to continue their work.

All in all it appears reasonable to attribute some portion of the superior achievement of pupils from the Group-Investigation classes to a distinct increase in their motivation to learn and to the heightened interest in and attention to the task that result from their motivation. The findings reported here are consistent with the position we took in earlier research that significant improvement in achievement with cooperative learning is not dependent on the use of rewards that are external to the group learning process itself (Sharan, 1980, 1984). Indeed, we are inclined to speculate that the kind of motivation stimulated by external rewards, and the kind fostered by the social-intellectual environment created by the Group-Investigation approach, may very well be two completely different kinds of motivation whose differences are not fully captured by the terms 'extrinsic' and 'intrinsic.'

Levels or Kinds of Achievement

The reader should recall that the Group-Investigation method is not merely a set of instructional techniques but it embodies an entire philosophy of education. It is based upon philosophical and psychological principles that differ fundamentally from those that underlie the prevailing style of instructional practice (Sharan and Hertz-Lazarowitz, 1980; Sharan and Sharan, 1976). The proper implementation of this approach entails a major change in the nature of the pupils' school experience. This change can lead not only to more learning but to a superior level or kind of learning as well. The components of this higher-level learning are inherent in the variables studied here in addition to the formal assessment of academic knowledge, namely in their social interaction (Tables 8-13) and their verbal behavior (Tables 16-21).

Schools strive, albeit mostly in theory but little in practice, to cultivate positive and productive interpersonal relations among pupils, as well as to develop their ability to communicate with others in a meaningful fashion. Thus, the data obtained on all of the measures used in this study can be viewed as constituting different dimensions of student achievement. That term should not be applied to scores derived exclusively from tests of subject-matter knowledge. However, the achievement data themselves provide some key to understanding how the Group-Investigation method enhances the pupils' level of learning. This key is found in the distinction between High and Low-Level achievement.

The experiment reported here is the third study in which the distinction between high and low level cognition served as a guide in the preparation of the achievement test. In the first study (Sharan, Ackerman and Hertz-Lazarowitz, 1980), the pupils were in grades 2 through 6. Those who had studied in classes using the Group-Investigation approach achieved higher scores than their peers from the Whole-Class classes on the high-level, but not on the low-level questions. A second experiment with 7th grade pupils in junior high schools also found that pupils from the Group-Investigation classes got higher scores on the high-level questions in the study of Literature than their peers in the same schools who were in the Whole-Class method (Sharan, Bejarano, Kussell and Peleg, 1984). Surprisingly, the pupils in the Whole-Class classes received higher scores on the low-level questions than the Group-Investigation students.

The study presented here is the first to yield higher achievement scores for the Group-Investigation pupils on both low and high-level questions, by contrast with pupils from the classrooms taught with the Whole-Class approach. This three-time 'replication' of the finding that Group-Investigation pupils excel in responding to higher-level questions about the subject matter they studied provides a basis for concluding that the Group-Investigation method fosters a more complex intellectual approach to academic subject matter than does teacher-directed, Whole-Class instruction. Moreover, it seems that this contribution to pupils' intellectual functioning in regard to academic subject matter need not be achieved at the expense of acquiring 'low-level' information, at least not when the Group-Investigation method is implemented with a reasonable degree of faithfulness to its principles and procedures (which are, of course, not always realized in practice). We may conclude, therefore, that, in addition to increased motivation and interest, pupils in the Group-Investigation method are likely to engage in a serious and high-level examination of the topic they are studying, from which they appear to derive considerable benefit.

Achievement and the Pupils' Social and Verbal Behavior

The findings obtained in this study about the pupils' social and verbal behavior shed light on what may occur in groups of pupils who had been exposed to either of the two teaching methods when they engage in a discussion of academic subject matter. We cannot be certain that the same patterns of interaction and verbal behavior characterized the behavior of these pupils when they were in their study groups in the classroom, or that the patterns displayed by the pupils from the Whole-Class method emerged at any time during the conduct of their learning procedures that did not include any group context. We can only assume that the 30-minute discussions of the 27 groups that were filmed toward the end of the 5-month period during which they studied in cooperative groups did not differ significantly from the behavioral patterns typical of the students' interaction in the Group-Investigation classes on other days. We must also remember that the filmed discussions document the pupils' speech, while the achievement scores derive from written tests, and that these two forms of assessing knowledge are very different. Finally we must indicate that the achievement scores reported here were compiled from the scores of over 350 pupils in the study whereas the films were made of 128 pupils in groups of 6 who were selected at random from the various classes. We will address ourselves to these topics again in a later section of this discussion, in conjunction with our examination of the 'process-outcome' relationship between the social and verbal behavior displayed during the discussions and the pupils' scores on the achievement tests.

What must be recalled at this time is the fact that all of the data in this study about the pupils' social and verbal behavior, pupils from both the Group-Investigation and Whole-Class methods, were obtained from films of group discussions. These films provided a record of 100% of the pupils' behavior during the discussions. The research performed heretofore on social interaction among pupils who had experienced cooperative learning in their classrooms relied on verbal self reports or on samples of pupils' behavior recorded by observers at time intervals (Sharan, Raviv et al, 1984). In the present study, all pupils from both teaching methods displayed considerable capacity for behaving cooperatively with one another, and for restricting their non-cooperative interaction, as is evident in the findings. Even in this situation, some important differences emerged between those pupils who had studied in the Group-Investigation and Whole-Class methods. The most salient finding is that the pupils from Middle-Eastern background received as high a frequency of cooperative statements from their Western classmates as did the Western children in these groups. Also, there was a balance of cooperative statements addressed by the Western children to other Western and to Middle-Eastern children in the groups from the cooperative learning classes. In the Whole-Class classes the Western children received far more cooperative statements than the Middle-Eastern pupils from both the Western and from the Middle-Eastern pupils in their groups, while the Middle-Eastern pupils received very few such statements. True, relatively few cooperative statements were addressed to the Middle-Eastern pupils by other Middle-Eastern students in the Group-Investigation classes as well. However, the frequency of cooperative statements addressed to Middle-Eastern pupils in the Group-Investigation classes was still significantly higher than those addressed to Middle-Eastern students in the Whole-Class method.

Of course, the finding of greater symmetry in cooperative interaction among pupils from the different ethnic groups who had studied in the Group-Investigation classes is an important finding in its own right, in terms of the social goals of the multiethnic classroom. This finding coincides with earlier reports of greater interethnic cooperation fostered by cooperative learning classes compared to traditionally taught classes (Hertz-Lazarowitz, Sharan and Steinberg, 1980; Sharan, Raviv, et al, 1984; Sharan and Rich, 1984). We surmise that these conditions prevailed in the small groups that operated in the Group-Investigation classes during their regular classroom learning activities, and that the greater cooperation among all students in the small groups contributed to the students' higher level of academic achievement. Although the Middle-Eastern students were the ones who received more cooperative statements in the Group-Investigation classes than in the Whole-Class method, participation in the cooperative groups obviously benefited all of the students in terms of their formal academic achievement. The relationship between peer cooperation in the group and pupils' academic achievement is also documented by the significant results obtained by the regression analyses reported in this experiment (to be discussed later in this chapter).

A similar pattern of findings appears in the data about the pupils' quantity of speech. Pupils from both the Western and Middle-Eastern Jewish ethnic groups who came from the Group-Investigation classes spoke more in their discussion groups than the pupils from the Whole-Class method. Thus, there was more intensive communication in groups formed from the former classes than from the latter ones. It follows that everyone participated more actively in the groups from the Group-Investigation classes. Since the Middle-Eastern pupils spoke more often in the discussion groups from the Group-Investigation classes, inevitably the Western pupils in these groups were able to speak less often. Only then could there be a greater symmetry in the number of times pupils from each ethnic group could speak. This symmetry between Western and Middle-Eastern pupils in the quantity of their speech points to a more equitable social status enjoyed by the Middle-Eastern pupils in the Group-Investigation classes (Cohen, 1980; Cohen and Sharan, 1980). In addition to the question of status, it also means that the Middle-Eastern pupils expressed themselves more often and could contribute more to their groups. Even though the Western pupils spoke somewhat fewer times (though not significantly fewer!), the total number of turns to speak in the discussion taken by the pupils from the Group-Investigation classes was not less but more than the number of turns in the groups selected from the Whole-Class method. Again we surmise that the high rate of speech found in the small groups that functioned in the Group-Investigation classes contributed to the pupils' noteworthy performance on the achievement tests.

Findings about the extent of the pupils' individualistic behavior, the extent to which they addressed their statements to the group as a whole and not only to individuals in the group, and the extent of their confused behavior in the discussion groups, should not be overlooked. On all of these measures, the pupils from the Group-Investigation classes emerged as superior to their peers from the Whole-Class method, as is to be expected (Tables 12 and 13). These findings mean that the pupils from both ethnic groups learned to work cooperatively with their peers in the Group-Investigation classes and to organize their learning effort on their own without teacher intervention. Just how important the experience in the Group-Investigation classes was for the pupils from Middle-Eastern background can be learned by comparing the mean scores on the measure of 'Confusion' (Table 12, category 9) for the pupils who came from the Group-Investigation with those from the Whole-Class method (11.28 in the Whole-Class method compared to 6.32 for the Middle Eastern pupils who came from the Group-Investigation method). These scores, along with the results about the quantity of speech, should give us some appreciation of the extent to which the Group-Investigation classes provided the pupils from Middle-Eastern background with a sense of involvement in the learning process and of not being left out because they could not compete with others in the class. The Middle-Eastern pupils talked to the group as a whole as often as did the Western pupils and were neither more nor less disconnected from the group's work (Confusion) as were their Western groupmates. On these measures as well, pupils from both ethnic groups in the Group-Investigation classes displayed a symmetry in their behavior that was

127

absent in the behavior of the pupils from the Whole-Class method where the Middle-Eastern students appeared to be less involved in the group discussion. If the pupils of Middle-Eastern background are equally disconnected from the learning process that occurs in the traditionally taught classrooms, where they are not even encouraged or allowed to interact directly with their classmates but required to listen at length to the teacher, it is clear how the findings reported in this study provide some explanation as to why these pupils achieved higher scores on the tests of academic achievement in the classes taught with the Group-Investigation method.

Cognitive Strategies and Pupils' Achievement

Using again the data from the group discussions as an indication of the kind of discourse that occurred in the cooperative groups during their classroom learning activities, it appears that the groups from the Group-Investigation classes conducted their activities at a relatively high level of intellectual functioning. It was certainly a higher level than the one displayed by the pupils from the Whole-Class classes when they were asked to conduct group discussions. It is altogether possible, and even likely, that instruction in the Whole-Class method was conducted by the teachers in this very prestigious school at a fairly high level of discourse. However, the results obtained in this study suggest that, even if the instruction by the teacher was at a high level, the Middle-Eastern pupils do not seem to have made these patterns of communication

128

part of their own repertoire. The relative absence of direct peer interaction focused on the subject matter in the Whole-Class method appears to result in the fact that the lower-class pupils hear the teachers' language but do not learn it. Teaching and learning are often parallel processes that interrelate less than we would be inclined to admit. Pupils may listen to teachers' use of verbal and cognitive strategies, but these do not necessarily impact on the pupils in any discernible fashion. The comparison made in this study between the effects of the two teaching methods suggests that the lower-class Middle-Eastern pupils were more likely to adopt verbal-intellectual patterns or strategies that they themselves used or experienced in their own communications than the patterns they only heard in the teachers' speech.

The conclusions reached here are, of course, not new to educators concerned with language policy in schools. Of the many works on this subject that support the argument proposed here, we shall quote one passage written close to two decades ago. After study of language usage by pupils in some of England's secondary schools, Barnes wrote:

"Here lies the importance of pupil participation. It is when the pupil is required to use language to grapple with new experience in a new way that he is most likely to find it necessary to use language differently. And this will be very different from taking over someone else's language in external imitation of its forms: on the contrary, it is the first step towards new patterns of thinking and feeling, new ways of representing reality to himself ... . It is not enough for pupils to imitate the forms of teachers' language as if they were models to be copied: it is only when they 'try it out' in reciprocal exchanges so that they modify the way they use language to organize reality that they are able to find new functions for language in thinking and feeling" (Barnes, 1969, 61-62).

Barnes' observations are consistent with the findings reported in this study about the cognitive strategies revealed in the speech of the Middle-Eastern pupils from the Group-Investigation classrooms compared to that of their ethnic peers from the Whole-Class method. We will return later in this discussion to the subject of the data from the various kinds of cognitive strategies when we consider their implications for understanding children's language in multiethnic classrooms. Here we wish to observe that the lower-class, Middle-Eastern pupils employed these kinds of cognitive strategies more frequently than their ethnic peers from the Whole-Class method. Hence, their increased participation in the group discussions revealed in the quantity of speech means that they probably made intellectually valuable contributions to these discussions, and that the quantity of speech included high-level contributions and not just a larger flow of words. The Middle-Eastern children had comments of substance to contribute to the group discussions. We assume that they had at least equally meaningful comments to make in their classrooms during their participation in the small groups. Just what these comments were and how they relate to the substantive issues discussed in the groups must await a detailed content analysis of the children's speech, as linguisitc ethnographers have pointed out (Mehan, 1979). The Group-Investigation method thus provides the kind of classroom learning environment that many educators concerned with language policy and development have long advocated but have yet to implement.

It is important to recall again that the verbal behavior of the pupils from the Whole-Class method was being studied as it manifested itself in a group discussion, under the very same conditions in which the discussions took place with the pupils from the Group-Investigation method. Yet, in their actual classrooms, pupils in the Whole-Class method do not typically engage in discussions in groups of 6 where communication among the students is direct and not mediated by the teacher. The group setting that was filmed for this study thus afforded pupils from the Whole-Class method the social conditions of small-group interaction that are conducive to more intimate and freer communication that ordinarily do not occur in their regular classrooms. Consequently, the pupils' verbal behavior displayed in the films may be distinctly superior to the patterns of communication that they would ordinarily use when studying in classes conducted with the Whole-Class method. All of the reasons cited here could have contributed to the lower achievement scores of the students in the Whole-Class method.

The Relationship between the Discussions and Academic Achievement

Investigators of cooperative learning have been aware of the need to examine the interaction among group members as the group carries out its collective task. The goal of such research is to determine how the events that occur as the group proceeds with its work influence the nature of the groups' final products, particularly the level of academic achievement of the groups' members. This kind of research has focused on the internal dynamics of cooperative groups' (Johnson and Johnson, 1985), and on the 'process-outcome' relationship (Webb, 1985). On occasion one hears versions of the claim that pupils advance their achievement in small groups because the 'smart' members of the group simply help the less able students, while the group as a unit doesn't really contribute anything to the pupils' achievement beyond the one-to-one 'peer-tutoring' interaction.

Many social and cognitive processes have been identified that occur more frequently in cooperative groups than in the Whole-Class method (Johnson and Johnson, 1985). However, one of the main difficulties in establishing the relationship between high frequencies of particular behavioral patterns, either social or cognitive, and academic achievement does not seem to have been overcome. That difficulty is how to specify the causal link between process and product. Students in a cooperative group reported that they employed higher level cognitive processes than did students working individually (Johnson and Johnson, 1981), but that finding was not directly related to those students' achievement except by inference. Establishing such causal links poses a difficult challenge for research, one that probably requires very complex techniques to overcome. Webb's studies (1985) did relate processes directly to outcomes, and her work should stimulate more research on this topic. To date, however, the process-product data are very limited in scope. They dealt primarily with sets of simple problems that have unequivocal answers, such as in mathematics, and the study of group interaction has been limited to the giving and receiving of help specific to a particular kind of problem. The nature and effects of controversy (Johnson and Johnson, 1979; Smith, Johnson and Johnson, 1981), and of the free exchange of ideas as occurs in groups, and not just giving and receiving the right answers or explanations of these answers, are only a few of the many topics that remain largely unexplored in terms of their relationship to group outcomes of various kinds. How particular interpersonal exchanges in a group are related to its solution of a problem, is a very complex subject to study. In our estimation, we still know relatively little about the relationship between various types of interactions in cooperative learning groups and the nature of the intellectual products of these groups, including their academic achievement. We know that these interactions help pupils learn, but we do not really know HOW that is accomplished in most learning situations. More detailed knowledge about the interpersonal processes in cooperative groups that foster higher levels of achievement, including the types of social and intellectual functions that were analyzed in the experiment reported here, could direct our efforts to cultivate those processes and to make the design and implementation of cooperative learning more effective.

The present experiment does not claim to have solved the problem of how to study process-product relationships. A field experiment is subject to many constraints, and we were unable to overcome several impediments to process-product research that have plagued other investigators. The administrative and organizational conditions in schools where studies of this kind are carried out frequently cancel the investigators' best-laid plans whether they like it or not. Our original plan for investigating the process-product relationships in this experiment called for having the pupils reply to a special achievement test immediately after we filmed the discussion session. In this way we thought it would be possible to relate the data obtained from the discussion with the pupils' academic knowledge. The plan proved to be unworkable for two reasons: First, it was imperative to employ a uniform achievement test. However, only two groups could be videotaped at a given time and students taking the test would then be free to inform their classmates about its contents. Second, we could not arrange to have students tested after the conclusion of the filming because they had to go to another class. As a result of these and other factors, we had to rely on the achievement tests administered before and after the experimental period to supply the "products" that we wished to relate to the processes that occurred during the group discussions. These discussions took place weeks before the post-test examinations. Also, the discussions were purely verbal exchanges while the examinations were written tests, and, of course, the examinations were individual tests while the processes occurred in a group environment. All of these features, that distinguish the group discussion context from the individual achievement examination, certainly affected the degree to which a relationship could emerge in the statistical analysis between the process data and the scores on the achievement tests.

Despite all of these limitations on the data from which we calculated the process-product relationship in this study, the results of the multiple regression analyses were surprisingly significant though modest in size (Table22). These analyses employed all of the measures of group process used in this study and related them to the achievement scores that the same pupils obtained on the questions assessing Low and High-Level intellectual functioning on the Geography and on the History tests. The measures of group process were: cooperative interactions (Categories 1, 2, and 3 in Table 8); measures of group controversy (Categories 4, 5, and 6 in Table 10); the number of words spoken and number of turns of speech taken during the discussion (Table 16); the six categories of focused interactions of verbal behavior (Table 18); and the data from the nine categories of intellectual functioning (Table 20). These six measures, all scored from the discussions held by the groups selected from the classrooms taught with the Group-Investigation or Whole-

Class methods were entered into step-wise, multiple regression analyses, following fathers' level of education, as the independent variables to predict the variance in the achievement scores from low and high level questions separately on each of the two post tests (History and Geography). Each of the four analyses yielded statistically significant results that accounted for sizeable portions of the variance in the achievement scores. On the low and high level questions in Geography, the process measures accounted for 15% and 8%, respectively, of the variance, and for 5% of the variance in the low level and 5% in the high level questions in History.

These findings support the assertion made here that the process variables are related to the pupils' knowledge as evaluated by written achievement tests. This was true even though the achievement tests tapped a very limited range of the pupils' knowledge compared to the open-ended discussions they could carry on in their small groups. Furthermore, there are marked differences between social and verbal interaction in discussions, and written tests of achievement, so that the continuity between these two situations was very attenuated. Consequently, the results obtained here appear to reflect a fairly strong and positive relationship between group processes and academic learning in school. We conjecture that the group processes predict a much larger portion of the pupils' knowledge of subject matter than was found in the regression analyses, inpart because only some of this knowledge was tapped by the achievement tests. It is reasonable to assume that the pupils learned and understood many ideas that they were not asked or able to express on the achievement test.

These ideas might have played an important role in the group discussions. It is possible that the disparity in content between the topic of the discussions and the questions on the achievement test had some effect on the process-product relations found in this study, above and beyond the differences between these two situations that were mentioned above.

The data obtained here emphasize that the nature of the interaction that occurs as a group proceeds with its task cannot be captured by, or reduced to, giving or receiving the right answers. When pupils are afforded the opportunity to maintain multilateral communication in a learning group, and the task allows for a broad range of intellectual perspectives on the topic, pupils display a rich variety of intellectual, verbal and social behavior (Schmuck and Schmuck, 1983). Research about the effects of instructional methods should embody at least some semblance of the complexity that we anticipate in those effects if we are to obtain valid knowledge regarding the impact of instruction. Over-simple measures of pupil behavior in classroom settings creates the misleading impression that educational experiences have similarly superficial effects on childrens' lives.

Verbal Behavior

Our discussion thus far dealt with the various findings in this study in terms of their possible contribution to the pupils' academic achievement. The effects of the two teaching methods on the pupils' verbal behavior have many implications independent of considerations about

137

achievement. The question we address here is: What is the meaning of the effects found in this experiment on the pupils' verbal behavior? And, how can we understand these effects for pupils from each of the two ethnic groups?

Frequency of Speech

Of central significance are the findings about the frequency of the pupils' speech (Tables 16 and 17). The two instructional methods exerted differential effects on the pupils' speech: The Western pupils in groups from the Group-Investigation method took fewer turns to speak and the Middle-Eastern pupils took more turns to speak than their ethnic peers in the discussion groups formed with pupils from the Whole-Class method. This is true even though the Western pupils continued to say more words per speaking turn than the Middle-Eastern pupils, and despite the fact that both the Western and Middle-Eastern pupils employed more words per turn of speech in the groups from the Group-Investigation than from the Whole-Class classes. The emergence of a relatively symmetrical frequency of speech between members of the two ethnic groups from the Group-Investigation classes stands in sharp contrast to the asymmetrical frequencies displayed in the groups from the traditional Whole-Class method. As was noted before, despite the decline in the number of turns taken in the discussion by the Western pupils from the Group-Investigation classes, the total number of turns of speech that emerged in the discussions held by pupils from the Group-Investigation classes was not smaller, and even slightly larger than the total number of turns taken in the

138

discussions held by pupils from the Whole-Class method. Along with the larger number of words used by pupils from the Group-Investigation classes, this finding about the greater symmetry in turns of speech between members of the different ethnic groups certainly can be interpreted as reflecting a distinct difference between the effects of the two teaching methods on the way pupils interact with one another and on the way this interaction affects their opportunity for participating in the learning process.

The frequency of speech in a discussion is a matter of considerable importance for understanding the relationship between the partners to the discussion. Theoreticians of children's language in social settings have claimed that each turn of speech during a discussion is intended to enforce a degree of control by the speaker over the discussion (Austin, 1962; Searle, 1969, 1979). Turns of speech, known as "illocutionary force," appear to constitute an important component in regulating the relationship and distribution of speaking turns in a discussion. In the groups from the Whole-Class method there was a very large gap between the two ethnic groups in favor of the Western pupils who clearly controlled the verbal exchange in the groups. This situation in the discussion groups can be viewed as reflecting the relationship between the ethnic groups in the traditional classroom. The bulk of the interpersonal processes, including compilation of information, interpreting messages and evaluation of statements (Borman, 1969) was dominated by the Western pupils in the groups from the Whole-Class method, whereas the symmetry between the ethnic groups was restored in the discussion groups from the Group-Investigation classes.

One may assume that the practice pupils had experienced with small-group dynamics in the Group-Investigation classrooms resulted in their establishing a more equitable division of control over their verbal behavior among all members of the group (Sharan, 1984; Sharan and Sharan, 1976). This symmetry in the frequency of speech can also be interpreted as reflecting a relatively equal social status situation by comparison to the status conditions in the groups from the Whole-Class method, as we shall discuss later in this section.

The frequency of speech in discussions appears to play a role in children's intellectual functioning and development, as well as in their status relationships with peers. Ever since Piaget's (1926) early writings about children's language, much research has been directed at exploring the relationship between language and thinking in children. Obviously, that topic goes beyond the central concern of the present experiment which is the effect of two instructional methods on children's verbal behavior. In short we can note that research supports the conclusion that conversations among peers, as well as between adults and children, can contribute significantly to children's intellectual development (Britton, 1970; Chang and Wells, 1987; Smith, 1960; Wells, 1986). Consequently we may conclude that the frequency of speech, both the number of turns spoken and the number of words, can have importance for children's development in general and for those from the minority or lower-class groups in particular.

Research on children's language from different ethnic groups often has assumed that there is a relationship between language and academic achievement (Bereiter and Engleman, 1966; Bernstein, 1971). An entire school of thought regarding children's language in school asserted that minority-group and/or lower-class children's language was limited or even impoverished in terms of its communication codes, and, as a result, the children's academic achievement was also impaired (Stahl, 1977). This fundamental premise about lower-class children's language deficiency created the expectation among teachers that pupils from families who had come to Israel from the countries of the Middle-East are capable of only limited participation in class discussions and that their ability to comprehend the transactions in the classroom was also very restricted. Thus, they occupied a lower academic as well as social status in the classroom. (See the discussions in Eshel and Klein, 1984; Stubbs, 1983).

The expectation that minority-group children are capable of limited understanding and participation in classroom learning has been approached from the point of view of status theory and expectation theory, both of which bear upon the issue of these children's verbal behavior in multiethnic classroom settings. In her research on cross-ethnic interaction in groups, Elizabeth Cohen employed the frequency of verbal participation as a measure of status (Cohen, 1972, 1980). She found that pupils in multiethnic groups who did not know each other in school and, hence, had no knowledge about each other's academic performance, still shared the expectation that the minority-group children would participate less frequently, and would influence the group's decisions less than would pupils from the majority group. These expectations exerted decisive influence on the pupils' verbal behavior during the performance of the groups' task. Results similar to those obtained in the United States were found in Israel (Cohen and Sharan, 1980).

In the experiment described here, the status relations obtaining in the discussion groups were more complex and overdetermined than those prevailing in the groups studied in earlier research. In the present research the pupils in the discussion groups all studied together in the same classroom and knew each other well, thus creating what has been termed a 'multi-characteristic status situation' (Berger, Fisek, Norman and Zelditch, 1977). In this latter case, the participants categorize each other (knowingly or unknowingly) not only by their ethnic or social class membership, which alone exerts considerable influence on their expectations about each others' potential contribution to their collective group effort, but they have much information about each other's academic abilities as well, as these were manifested in daily classroom life. Such doubly reinforced social categorization is particularly resistant to change (Brewer and Miller, 1984). Expectations of this kind are what await minority-group or lower-class pupils in the multiethnic classroom, expectations that are shared by teachers and peers alike. The consequences of these expectations, whether they stem from the condition of being a disadvantaged lower-class learner who suffers from impoverished communication codes, or from the negative effects of status expectations, are what emerged here in the data about the pupils' frequency of speech in the discussion groups selected from the Whole-Class classes (Table 16). As we noted before, this glaring imbalance in social status is absent in the groups from the Group-Investigation

142

classrooms, at least in terms of the frequency of the pupils' speech, and the groups displayed a fairly symmetrical pattern of quantity of speech.

In light of the interpretations offered thus far, the data from the Group-Investigation classes regarding the pupils' frequency of speech can be understood as indicating a far more equitable set of status relations among members of the two ethnic groups, than those prevailing in the groups selected from the traditional classrooms. Pupils accustomed to collaborating with one another in small groups established a different pattern of interethnic relations than the pattern characterizing the peer interaction in the groups from the Whole-Class method. These findings thus reveal the far-reaching effect of the instructional methods on the pupils' verbal behavior, and, consequently, on the nature of their peer relationships (Cohen, 1986).

Another important perspective from which to view the findings about the number of turns of speech taken by the pupils is that of the teacher and the instructional approach to which he/she is accustomed. There are data to show that teachers using the Whole-Class method frequently relate pupils' use of complete and well-formed, grammatical sentences to the pupils' academic status (Mehan, 1980). Teachers in Israel have been observed to correct their pupils' use of language almost automatically if they speak in a non-standard fashion (Eiger, 1975; Shapiro, 1981; Stahl, 1977). It is possible that the pupils in the discussion groups from the Whole-Class method continued in their teachers' footsteps and related more to those members of the group who spoke in the academically acceptable fashion. Pupils in the Group-Investigation groups learned to cooperate, and argue, with peers regardless of their ethnic, social class or language characteristics because they were all working together for a common group goal. Observers of children's conversations in schools have noted that pupils working together in groups often increase their sensitivity to the feedback they receive from other children in their group, and they learn to take their partners' communicational needs into consideration during the discussion (Eisenberg and Garvey, 1981; Labov and Fanshel, 1977).

In the study reported here, an effect for instructional method emerged on only one of the six categories of 'focused interactions,' namely the category of 'interruptions.' Pupils in the Group-Investigation classes learned to interrupt each other less than pupils from the Whole-Class method. However the pupils' experience in the different learning methods had no other discernible effect on their verbal behavior as measured by these categories. It seems that these fundamental forms of speech are not influenced by instruction, at least not over periods of time such as the relatively short duration of this experiment. Dorval and Eckerman (1984) found significant changes in the use of these categories in the speech of children and adults at different age levels, so the frequency with which these categories appear in spontaneous conversations does increase during the course of time. The groups of subjects whose language was studied were separated by three or four years or more. This experiment included only one age group and took place over a period of five months. Moreover, the experiment was not directed specifically at altering the pupils' patterns of speech. Hence it is not

144

altogether surprising that significant changes in the use of these categories were not evident in the pupils' discussions.

The data presented here about the pupils' verbal communication after having experienced cooperative learning or Whole-Class methods of instruction stem from only one approach to the study of children's discourse. Other approaches, such as linguistic and ethnographic analyses of the content of the speech and of its sequential features, could, potentially, yield a completely different view of how the children's talk was affectd by their classroom experience (Cazden, 1986; Mehan, 1979). Such analyses might also produce valuable insights into differential patterns of discouse typical of pupils from the different ethnic groups, if, in fact, such divergent patterns exist. The authors hope to subject the videotape records of the group discussions to further study in the future.

Cognitive Strategies

Pupils of Middle-Eastern background from the Group-Investigation classes used many of these categories more frequently than their ethnic peers from the Whole-Class method (Table 20). There were no significant differences found in the use of these categories by pupils from Western background who had studied in one or the other instructional methods. This finding means that the discussion groups from the Group-Investigation classes employed a higher level of discourse than the groups from the Whole-Class method. This is not to imply, as we have stressed before, that the use of more intellectual categories in speech indicates a higher level of mental ability, only a more developed communicative effectiveness within the system of expectations prevailing in the school (Shimron, 1984; Stubbs, 1983).

The fact that the pupils from the Middle-Eastern or lower-class families who studied in the Group-Investigation classes also demonstrated a higher level of discourse than their ethnic peers in the Whole-Class method does not imply that they expressed themselves in a style not typically used in their daily lives. Research on the use of dialects by minority groups generally shows that being exposed to standard speech, even for extended periods of time, exerts little effect on language acquisition and usage by pupils who ordinarily do not employ the standard forms of speech (Cazden, Bryant and Tillman, 1972). We do not wish to draw any simple parallels between the nature of the language usage and cognitive functioning by Middle-Eastern Jewish children in Israel and that of lower-class children from various ethnic groups in other countries (Davis, 1978). Nevertheless, there appear to be several salient differences in language usage between children from Jewish families who came to Israel from the various countries of the Middle-East and who are also from the lower economic status group, and those children whose families came from Europe, the English-speaking countries and South America. Such differences have been observed in the relatively less frequent use of formal codes and registers (Davis, 1977, 1978; Nir, 1976; Rabin, 1982), as well as in the more prominent use of metaphoric rather than descriptive language (Shimron, 1984) in the speech of lower-class children from Middle-Eastern background in

Israel. Thus, the greater frequency of cognitive strategies in the language of the children from Middle-Eastern background who studied in the Group-Investigation classes, as well as the relative symmetry between the two ethnic groups in the frequency of their turns of speech, compared to the children from the Whole-Class method, testifies to the fact that the group discussions with pupils from the Group-Investigation classrooms were not dominated so blatantly by a particular language code. Rather, it seems that the two codes prevailed side by side. In cooperative learning classes all pupils listened to the children from Middle-Eastern background for relatively extended periods of time (Table 8) and it may be that the prolonged collaboration reduced the salience or importance of the language differences between members of the two groups. Pupils from the Middle-Eastern group seem to have gained legitimacy for their own language code in this setting along with the code typical of Western middle-class pupils. We might add that the category of 'listening to respond' (Table 8) appeared more frequently in the statements addressed to both Western and by Middle-Eastern pupils to their groupmates from Middle-Eastern background. Indeed, pupils from Middle-Eastern background listened to each other almost twice as much when they had studied in the Group-Investigation classes than when they came from the Whole-Class classes. Still, as Shimron (1984) observed, Western pupils listen to others more than their schoolmates from the Middle-Eastern group, regardless of which teaching method they had experienced.

These interpretations are consistent with what Dell Hymes (1972) wrote about the evaluative-judgemental approach to different language codes:

"It is not that a child does not know the word, but he pronounces it in one social dialect rather than in the other. Not that a child cannot express himself or that a thought cannot be required of him, but that he expresses it in one style of expression rather than another."

This statement was addressed to teachers. The pupils in our study appear to have applied it in practice in a setting where their spoken language did not serve as a criterion for their academic status, and where the group focused its attention on performing its task.

Research into the causes of lower-class children's low academic performance has often attributed this phenomenon to their use of a non-standard language. There are, of course, other theories regarding the relationship between language and thought that have proposed alternative explanations for children's success or failure in school (Chomsky, 1965; Macnamara, 1972; Schlesinger, 1977; Stubbs, 1983; Vigotsky, 1962). There seems to be some agreement to the effect that spoken language gradually becomes an instrument of thought, and that this instrument is acquired by interaction between the individual and the environment (Solomon, 1981). We may conjecture that the children from Middle-Eastern background who studied in the Group-Investigation classes and who used many more of the cognitive strategies than did their ethnic peers in the Whole-Class method, were demonstrating the advance they had made in their use of language as an instrument in the service of their thinking processes by virtue of their having studied in these classes. Recent microlinguisitc research suggests that collaborative talk among peers in school can contribute to the improvement of children's higher-level problem solving thought processes (Chang and Wells, 1987). Again, our findings do not mean that pupils in the Group-Investigation classes displayed superior levels of thinking than pupils in the Whole-Class classes. The relationship between language and thought is too complex to be influenced directly by the changes studied here (Stubbs, 1983).

Findings about the pupils' use of 'concrete examples' also warrant some comment. In this category, the pupils from Middle-Eastern background received higher scores than their Western classmates. We should recall that, in the Group-Investigation classrooms, the pupils themselves selected the various sub-topics that the groups investigated as part of their study project. The pupils also decided how they would proceed with their work and how they planned to report the results of their work to the class as a whole (Sharan and Hertz Lazarowitz, 1980). This is precisely what some educators recommended as the preferred procedure for assisting lower-class pupils to improve their thinking skills, in particular their alleged deficit in abstract thinking (Eiger, 1975). We are not able to determine here the extent to which any of the pupils who participated in this experiment reached a higher level of abstraction in their thinking. The data gathered in this experiment strongly suggest that the pupils from Middle-Eastern background, who were also the lower-class pupils in this study, contributed a great deal to the group discussions, and that their contributions were accepted by all of their peers in the group without attracting special attention. There was no evidence of their being passive, intimidated or tolerated. Instead, they were full collaborators, active and involved in the group process, quantitatively and qualitatively.

Educational Environment as a Variable Affecting Children's Language

No specific steps were taken in this experiment to improve the children's language functioning, or to treat the Middle-Eastern children's alleged language 'deficits.' Yet, they, like their Western peers from the Group-Investigation classes, performed at a much higher level linguistically than the Middle-Eastern pupils in the Whole-Class method. This finding does not appear to be consistent with the theory that these children display a language deficit. True, this study also documents the presence of distinct differences in the frequency with which pupils from the two ethnic groups/social classes employ a variety of language strategies. Whether such differences constitute support for the theory that lower-class, Middle-Eastern children in Israel speak a different dialect of Hebrew than their Western peers is a question we must leave to linguists to consider. The fact that the Middle-Eastern pupils functioned in such a different fashion in the Group-Investigation classes than they did in the classes from the Whole-Class method suggests, as we have already argued, that the social setting in which pupils function in school exerts considerable influence on their verbal behavior. As such, it appears inappropriate to conclude that lower-class pupils' language as displayed in the traditional school setting reflects the full range of their communicative abilities.

An intensive and longitudinal study of young children's language at home and in school showed that the traditional school setting had a distinctly limiting effect on the quantity

151

and quality of the children's language by contrast with the same children's speech at home (Wells, 1986; see pages 84-87). The investigator noted that:

"But not only do the children speak less with an adult at school. In those conversations they do have, they get fewer turns, express a narrower range of meanings, and, in general, use grammatically less complex utterances. ....Teachers initiate a much higher proportion of conversations than parents do ... and ask a higher proportion of questions .... The result is that, at school children are reduced ... to the more passive role of respondent ....

Most significant of all in explaining the generally reduced level of competence that children show at school is the much more dominating role that teachers play in conversation .... Small wonder that some children have little to say or even appear to be lacking in conversational skills altogether ... schools are not providing an environment that fosters language development ...." (Wells, 1986, 87).

The results of the present experiment demonstrate that research on children's language must not ignore variation in the educational environment as a powerful influence on the children's language, and that it constitutes a critical factor that should not be treated as a constant as it has been heretofore. Research characterizing the patterns of verbal interaction in the classroom (Mehan, 1979), and the speech patterns of lower-class children in particular reflects the influence exerted by a specific kind of classroom experience over years of schooling, as much as it reflects

152

their lower-class or ethnic environment. When the learning environment is treated as a variable in research, as it was in the present study, distinctly different findings emerge. Of course, the cooperative learning method did not eradicate differences in language behavior between the two ethnic groups (Cais, 1984; Shimron, 1984). We do not claim that children from different cultural environments will function the same way, given the opportunity. Our assertion here, based on the data obtained in this study, and on theoretical considerations, is that the lower-class Middle-Eastern children can employ language to meet their needs and the needs of the school, even though they may do so differently than the children from Western background. That this is true is evident from the fact that in many of the categories of verbal behavior studied here the children of Middle-Eastern background in the Group-Investigation method performed equally as well, or even at a superior level, than did Western background children in the Whole-Class method. If teachers considered the performance of the Western children in the 'frontal' method classrooms as adequate, then the Middle-Eastern pupils in the Group-Investigation classes certainly could be evaluated as performing at an academically acceptable level without being judged as 'culturally deprived'. Such an evaluation is actually the only logical one given the findings reported here. Moreover, it is a necessary conclusion to be reached independent of the fact that the children of Middle-Eastern background continued to obtain lower scores than the Western background children in the same, i.e. Group-Investigation classes.

Contrary to the theory of cognitive deficit as an explanation for lower-class children's poor performance in school, Dell Hymes (1972) claimed that children whose language abilities were limited to those cultivated by the school, where schooling fails to allow them to develop and use their language abilities, are probably worse off than those children who allegedly suffer from cultural deprivation. When children's normal language abilities cannot find expression in school, one can speak of a condition of 'repression.' When the pupils from Middle-Eastern background participated in classrooms taught with the Group-Investigation method, they were free to communicate with each other with the wider range of verbal skills, to offer concrete examples of the ideas they were discussing, and to explain many ideas. Lower-class pupils from the classes taught with the Whole-Class approach were less able to employ these verbal-intellectual strategies. Therefore, what this study asserts is not so much that cooperative learning, during a five-month period, provided these children with the language skills they never had. Rather, it afforded a learning environment that allowed the children to give expression to a richer and wider range of language than school typically permits.

Summary

The experiment reported here was concerned with the effects of cooperative learning, through the Group-Investigation method, on pupils' academic achievement, on their social interaction with members of the other Jewish ethnic group in Israel and on the verbal behavior of pupils from the two ethnic groups, as these were displayed during the pupils' participation in a group discussion. Pupils' behavior in these domains was compared to that of their peers in the same school and grade level who had studied the same subject matter in the traditional Whole-Class format. The effect of instructional method on pupils' verbal performance should be of considerable interest to educators, particularly in light of the widely held view that lower-class children in Israel from Middle-Eastern ethnic background reach relatively low levels of academic achievement because, among other things, their language is very limited, and they can neither understand what occurs in classrooms nor participate on an equal footing with their classmates from Western ethnic background (middle-class). Given that lower-class pupils from Jewish families who came to Israel from countries of the Middle-East may express themselves somewhat differently than children from families of Western background, does this difference prevent them from participating actively in the classroom learning process, and how is their verbal performance affected by instructional practices? The experiment reported here bears on these questions.

Another topic that concerned the authors when planning this study was the degree of relationship between the interaction within the cooperative learning groups and the pupils' academic achievement. We calculated the relationship between the data obtained from relatively detailed analysis of social and verbal interaction during discussions held by small groups of pupils, and their scores on two tests of their academic achievement. In this fashion we sought to determine the extent to which the dynamics of the cooperative learning group contribute to the pupils' achievement, and, thereby, contribute to our understanding of the process-product relationship in cooperative learning groups. This kind of data is particularly vital in the case of teaching methods that place great emphasis on group-oriented process as the key to fostering improved learning outcomes.

In the present experiment, the academic achievement levels of the students from the Group-Investigation classes were far superior to those from the Whole-Class method on sets of questions that assessed both low and high-level uses of knowledge. This finding applies to pupils from both ethnic groups/social classes. In terms of academic achievement, all pupils in this experiment, from both Western and Middle-Eastern background, gained considerably from their participation in the cooperative learning classes. Social relations, measured by the number of cooperative statements and acts directed at pupils from the two ethnic groups, were far more equitable and symmetrical in the groups from the cooperative classes compared to those from the Whole-Class method where the Western pupils received much greater support from peers in their discussion groups than the Middle-Eastern pupils. Of particular interest is the fact that the Middle-Eastern pupils offered more support to their own ethnic peers after they had studied in Group-Investigation classes than in Whole-Class classes. In the latter groups, the Middle-Eastern pupils supported the dominant Western pupils much more than they supported each other. This state of affairs was not completely changed by the Group-Investigation method, but it was distinctly ameliorated (see Figure 3). Greater symmetry between the two ethnic groups in their verbal participation was evident in the frequency of the pupils' speech when they came from the Group-Investigation classes, whereas the dominance of the Western pupils in the Whole-Class method was obvious on this measure as well. Thus, the Group-Investigation classes appear to have generated more equalized status relations between the members of the two ethnic groups by contrast with the Whole-Class classe method. In these latter classes the Western group remains more blatantly dominant in social as well as in academic status.

Cooperative learning also affected positively the verbal behavior of the pupils from Middle-Eastern background. This was displayed by more frequent use of a set of cognitive strategies in the speech of the Middle-Eastern pupils from the Group-Investigation classes than was evident among pupils from the Whole-Class method. This finding suggests that the Middle-Eastern pupils were able not only to express themselves more often in the small cooperative groups, but that they also had a more significant contribution to make to the groups' progress than they were able to manage in the traditional classrooms. The cooperative small groups provided a more congenial and accepting environment in which the lower-class pupils could participate more freely and make fuller use of their verbal abilities than the traditional classroom. It seems more than apparent by now that this kind of educational environment is necessary for promoting the goals of integration in the multiethnic classroom. The traditional classroom is inhospitable to the lower-class pupils.

The data obtained here also suggest that the study of children's language should consider the nature of their educational experiences, and that these experiences exert significant effects on children's language above and beyond differences that can be attributed to their development in society at large over the course of years. We have no information at all about children's language development after several years of study in cooperative learning classrooms and how it might differ from that of peers who were exposed exclusively to the traditional classroom. We can only conjecture that the spontaneous usage of language in the two groups would be very different. We must emphasize again that the findings available thus far from the study of children's language development reflect a specific kind of schooling only. Investigators have drawn conclusions about language development that might require alteration when the pupil's experience in different educational environments is treated as a variable instead of as a constant. We should recall that this experiment did not treat the children's language per se, and there was no program of language enrichment or exercises. The regular curriculum in History and Geography was followed, except for the manner in which the students pursued their studies in the Group-Investigation method. Thus, the effects noted here stem directly from the reorganization of the social process that unfolds as the pupils pursue their tasks (Mehan, 1979). This reorganization has a far-reaching impact on pupils in many different realms of their experience, as numerous investigators of cooperative learning have studied and discussed (Slavin, Sharan, et al, 1985). The question that

158

remains for educators is not what to change to improve learning in school for countless children, but whether we want to change at all (Sarason, 1982, 1983). We have much evidence. We need an equal amount of will!

References

Ames, C., and Ames, R. (Eds.) Research on motivation in education, Vol. 2: The classroom milieu. Orlando, FL: Academic Press, 1985.

Austin, J. How to do things with words. London: Oxford University Press, 1962.

Bach, K. and Harnish, R. Linguistic communication and speech acts. Cambridge, MA: M.I.T. Press, 1979.

Bales, R. Interaction process analysis. Reading, Mass.: Addison-Wesley, 1950.

Baratz, J. and Shuy, R. (Eds.), Teaching black children to read. Washington, D.C.: Center for Applied Linguistics, 1969.

Barnes, D. Language in the secondary classroom. In: D. Barnes, J. Britton and H. Rosen (authors), Language, the learner and the school. Harmondsworth, England: Penguin, 1969.

Barnes, D. and Todd, F. Communication and learning in small groups. London: Routledge and Kegan-Paul, 1977.

Bereiter, C. and Engleman, S. Teaching disadvantaged children in the preschool. Englewood Cliffs, New Jersey: Prentice-Hall, 1966.

Berger, J., Fisek, M., Norman, R. and Zelditch, M. Status characteristics and social interaction. New York: Elsevier, 1977.

Bernstein, B. Class, codes and control. Vol. I, London: Routledge and Kegan Paul, 1971.

Bernstein, B. Education cannot compensate for society. In: D. Rubenstein and C.Stoneman (Eds.), <u>Education for democracy,</u> Harmondsworth, England: Penguin, 1972, 104-116.

Bernstein, B. <u>Class, codes and control</u>. Vol. 2, London: Routledge and Kegan Paul, 1973.

Borman, E. <u>Discussion and group methods</u>. New York: Harper and Row, 1969.

Brewer, M. and Miller, N. Beyond the contact hypothesis: Theoretical perspectives on desegregation. In: M. Brewer and N. Miller (Eds.), <u>Groups in contact</u>. New York: Academic Press, 1984, 281-302.

Britton, J. <u>Language and learning</u>. Harmondsworth, England: Penguin Books, 1970.

Cais, J. Socialization and verbal behavior: The language of disadvantaged and advantaged children. <u>Studies in Education</u>, 1978, 19, 131-152 (Hebrew).

Cais, J. Different Hebrew or bad Hebrew? <u>Studies in Education</u>, 1984, 40, 7-20, (Hebrew).

Cazden, C. Classroom discourse. In: M. Wittrock (Ed.), <u>Handbook of research on teaching</u> (3rd edition). New York: Macmillan, 1986, 432-463.

Cazden, C., Bryant, B. and Tillman, N. Making it and going home: The attitudes of black people toward language education. In: J. Griffeth and L. Miner (Eds.), <u>Proceedings of the 2nd and 3rd Lincoln land conferences on dialectology</u>. University of Alabama Press, 1972.

Chang, G. and Wells, G. The literate potential of collaborative talk. Paper presented at the International Oracy Convention, Norwich, England, April, 1987. (From Ontario Institute for Studies in Education, Toronto, Ontario, Canada).

Cherry, L. and Lewis, M. Mothers and two-year-olds: A study of sex differentiated aspects of verbal interaction. Developmental Psychology, 1976, 12, 278-282.

Chomsky, N. Aspects of the theory of syntax. Cambridge, Mass.: M.I.T. Press, 1965.

Cohen, E. Design and redesign of the desegregated school: problems of status, power and conflict. In: W. Stephan and J. Faegin (Eds.), School desegregation. New York: Plenum, 1980, 251-280.

Cohen, E. Interracial interaction disability. Human Relations, 1972, 25, 9-24.

Cohen, E. The desegregated school. In: N. Miller and M. Brewer (Eds.), Groups in contact: The psychology of desegregation. New York: Academic Press, 1984, 77-96.

Cohen, E. Designing groupwork. New York: Teachers College Press, 1986.

Cohen, E. and Sharan, S. Modifying status relations in Israeli youth. Journal of Cross-Cultural Psychology, 1980, 11, 364-384.

Cook, S. Cooperative interaction in multiethnic contexts. In: N. Miller and M. Brewer (Eds.), Groups in contact: The psychology of desegregation. New York: Academic Press, 1984, 155-185.

Cooper, C. How children help each other learn: Children's discourse in cooperative and didactic interaction. Paper presented at the annual convention of the American Educational Research Association, Boston, Mass.: April, 1980.

Cooper, C., Marquis, A. and Ayers-Lopez, S. Peer learning in the classroom: Tracing developmental patterns and consequences of children's spontaneous interactions. In: L. Wilkinson (Ed.), Communicating in the classroom. New York: Academic Press, 1982.

Davis, L. The language of culturally deprived children: Are they in need of 'treament'? Studies in Education, 1977, 14, 133-138, (Hebrew).

Davis, L. The register and the teaching of language to disadvantaged children. Studies in Education, 1978, 18, 61-66 (Hebrew).

DeCharms, R. Enhancing motivation: Change in the classroom. New York: Irvington Publishers (Halstead Press), 1976.

Donaldson, M. Children's minds. London: Fontana/Croom Helm, 1978.

Dorval, B. and Eckerman, C. Developmental trends in the quality of conversation achieved by small groups of acquainted peers. Monographs of the society for research in child development. 1984, 49, No. 2.

Eiger, H. Rehabilitative teaching for culturally deprived children. Tel-Aviv: Sifriat Poalim; 1975 (Hebrew).

Eisenberg, A. and Garvey, C. Children's use of verbal strategies in resolving conflicts. Discourse Processes, 1981, 4, 149-170.

163

Ervin-Tripp, S. Language acquisition and communicative choice. Palo Alto: Stanford University Press, 1972.

Eshel, Y. and Klein, Z. School desegregation and achievement. In: Y. Amir and S. Sharan (Eds.), School desegregation. Hillsdale, New Jersey: Lawrence Erlbaum, 1984, 133-153.

Feldstein, S. and Welkowitz, J. A chronography of conversation: in defense of the objective approach. In: A. Siegman and S. Feldstein (Eds.), Nonverbal behavior and communication. Hillsdale, New Jersey; Erlbaum, 1978.

Flavell, J., Botkin, P., Fry, C., Wright, J. and Jarvis, P. The development of role-taking and communication skills in children. New York: Wiley, 1968.

Frankenstein, K. Rehabilitating deficient intelligence. Jerusalem: The Hebrew University, 1972 (Hebrew).

Garvey, C. and Berninger, G. Turning and turn-taking in children's conversations. Discourse Processes, 1981, 4, 27-57.

Genishi, S. and De Paulo, M. Learning through argument in a pre-school. In: L.C.Wilkinson (Ed.), Communicating in the classroom. New York: Academic Press, 1982.

Gottman, J. and Parkhurst, J. A developmental theory of friendship and acquaintanceship processes. In: W. Collins (Ed.), The Minnesota symposia on child psychology (Vol.13). Hillsdale, New Jersey: Erlbaum, 1980.

164

Gumperz, J. Language in social groups. Palo Alto: Stanford University Press, 1971.

Halliday, M. Language as a social semiotic. London: Edward Arnold, 1979.

Hare, A.P. Handbook of small-group research. New York: Free Press, 2nd edition, 1976.

Hertz-Lazarowitz, R., Sharan, S., and Steinberg, R. Classroom learning style and cooperative behavior of elementary school children. Journal of Educational Psychology, 1980, 72, 97-104.

Hymes, D. Introduction. In: Cazden, C., John, V. and Hymes, D. (Eds.) Functions of language in the classroom. New York: Teachers College Press, 1972.

Hymes, D. Foundations in sociolinguistics: An ethnocraphic approach. Philadelphia: University of Pennsylvania Press, 1974.

Jacobs, S. Language. In: M. Knapp and G. Miller (Eds.), Handbook of interpersonal communication. Beverley Hills: Sage Publications, 1985, 313-343.

Johnson, D. and Johnson, R. Conflict in the classroom; controversy and learning. Review of Educational Research 1979, 49, 51-70.

Johnson, D. and Johnson, R. Effects of cooperative and individualistic learning experiences on interethnic interaction. Journal of Educational Psychology, 1981, 73, 454-459.

Johnson, D. and Johnson, R. The internal dynamics of cooperative learning groups. In: R.Slavin et al (Eds.) Learning to cooperate, cooperating to learn. New York: Plenum, 1985, 103-124.

Johnson, D. Johnson, R. and Maruyama, C. Interdependence and interpersonal attraction among heterogeneous and homogeneous individuals. Review of Educational Research, 1983, 53, 5-54.

Johnson, D., Maruyama, G., Johnson, R., Nelson, D. and Skon, L. Effects of cooperative, competitive, and individualistic goal structures on achievement: A meta-analysis. Psychological Bulletin, 1981, 89, 47-62.

Johnson, D., Skon, L. and Johnson, R. The effects of cooperative, competitive and individualistic goal structures on student achievement on different types of tasks. American Educational Research Journal, 1980, 17, 83-93.

Kagan, S., Zahn, L., Widaman, K., Schwarzwald, J. and Tyrrell, G. Classroom structural bias. In: R. Slavin, S. Sharan et al (Eds.) Learning to cooperate, cooperating to learn. New York: Plenum, 1985, 277-312.

Klein, L. and Eshel, Y. Integrating Jerusalem schools. New York: Academic Press, 1980.

Labov, W. The logic of non-standard English. In: F. Williams (Ed.), Language and poverty, Chicago: Markham, 1970.

Labov, W. and Fanshel, D. Therapeutic discourse. New York: Academic Press, 1977.

Littlewood, W. Communicative language teaching: An introduction. New York: Cambridge Univesity Press, 1981.

Macnamara, J. Cognitive basis of language learning in infants. Psychological Review, 1972, 79, 1-13.

Maruyama, G. Relating goal structures to other classroom processes. In: R. Slavin et at (Eds.), <u>Learning to cooperate, cooperating to learn</u>. New York: Plenum, 1985, 345-363.

Mehan, H. <u>Learning lessons</u>. Cambridge, Mass: Harvard University Press, 1979.

Mehan, H. The competent student. <u>Anthropology and Education Quarterly</u>, 1980, 11, 131-152.

Minkovitch, A. <u>The culturally deprived child</u>. Jerusalem: The Hebrew University, 1969 (Hebrew).

Nir, R. Towards a classification of errors in learning the mother-tongue. <u>Studies in Education</u>, 1976a, 13, 81-92 (Hebrew).

Nir, R. The concept of register and its place in the teaching of the mother-tongue. <u>Studies in Education</u>, 1976b, 11, 97-110 (Hebrew).

Piaget, J. <u>The language and thought of the child</u>. London: Routledge and Kegan Paul, 1952 (1926).

Rabin, C. Introduction to research on conversations. In: Blum-Kolka, S. Tubin, Y. and Nir, R (Eds.), <u>Studies in research on conversations</u>. Jerusalem, Akadimon Press, 1982 (Hebrew).

Rosaldo, M. The things we do with words: Plongot speech acts and speech act theory in philosophy. <u>Language in Society</u>, 1982, 11, 203-237.

Sacks, H., Schegloff, E. and Jefferson, G. A simplest semantics for the organization of turn-taking in conversation. <u>Language</u>, 1974, 50, 696-735.

Sarason, S. Schooling in America. New York: The Free Press, 1983.

Sarason, S. The culture of the school and the problem of change. Boston: Allyn and Bacon (2nd edition), 1982.

Schlesinger, I. The role of cognitive development and linguistic input in language acquisition. Journal of Child Language, 1977, 4, 153-169.

Schmuck, R. and Schmuck, P. Group processes in the classroom. Dubuque, Iowa: Brown, 1983 (4th edition).

Schwartzwald, 0. Grammar and reality in the Hebrew verb. Ramat-Gan: Bar-Ilan University, 1981 (Hebrew).

Searle, J. Speech acts. Cambridge: Cambridge University Press, 1969.

Searle, J. Expression and meaning. Cambridge: Cambridge University Press, 1979.

Shapira, D. A 'second chance' for culturally deprived children. Studies in Education, 1981, 30, 75-86 (Hebrew).

Sharan, S. Cooperative learning in small groups: Recent methods and effects on achievement, attitudes and ethnic relations. Review of Educational Research, 1980, 50, 241-271.

Sharan, S. Cooperative learning in the classroom: Research in desegregated schools. Hillsdale, New Jersey: Lawrence Erlbaum Associates, 1984.

Sharan, S., Bejarano, Y., Kussell, P. and Peleg, R. Achievement in English language and in literature. In: S. Sharan, Cooperative learning in the classroom: Research in desegregated schools. Hillsdale, New Jersey: Lawrence Erlbaum Associates, 1984, 46-72.

Sharan, S. and Hertz-Lazarowitz, R. A group-investigation method of cooperative learning in the classroom. In: S. Sharan et al (Eds.), Cooperation in education. Provo, Utah: Brigham Young University Press, 1980, 14-46.

Sharan, S., Hertz-Lazarowitz, R., and Ackerman, Z. Academic achievement of elementary school children in small-group versus whole-class instruction. Journal of Experimental Education, 1980, 48, 125-129.

Sharan, S., Hertz-Lazarowitz, R., and Reiner, T. Television for changing teacher behavior. Journal of Educational Technology Systems, 1978, 7, 119-131.

Sharan, S., Raviv, S., Kussell, P. and Hertz-Lazarowitz, R. Cooperative and competitive behavior. In: S. Sharan, Cooperative learning in the classroom. Hillsdale, N. Y.: Lawrence Erlbaum, 1984, 73-106.

Sharan, S., and Rich, Y. Field experiments on ethnic integration in Israeli schools. In: Y. Amir and S. Sharan (Eds.), School desegregation. Hillsdale, New Jersey: Lawrence Erlbaum, 1984, 189-217.

Sharan, S. and Sharan, Y. Small group teaching. Englewood Cliffs, New Jersey: Educational Technology Publications, 1976.

Sharan, S. and Shaulov, A. The effects of cooperative learning on pupils' motivation to learn, pro-social decision-making and social acceptance. Manuscript in preparation. School of Education, Tel-Aviv University, 1986.

Shimron, Y. Semantic development and communicative skills in different social classes. Discourse Processes, 1984, 7, 275-299.

Slavin, R. Cooperative learning. Review of Educational Research 1980, 50, 315-342.

Slavin, R. Cooperative learning. New York: Longman, 1983.

Slavin, R., Sharan, S., Kagan, S., Hertz-Lazarowitz, R., Webb, C. and Schmuck, R. (Eds.) Learning to cooperate, cooperating to learn. New York: Plenum, 1985.

Smith, A. A developmental study of group processes. The Journal of Genetic Psychology, 1960, 97, 29-39.

Smith, K., Johnson, D. and Johnson, R. Effects of controversy on learning in cooperative groups. Journal of Social Psychology, 1984, 122, 199-209.

Solomon, G. Communication. Tel-Aviv: Sifriat Poalim, 1981 (Hebrew).

Stahl, A. The structure of the written language of Western and Middle-Eastern background children in Israel. Unpublished Ph.D. dissertation. Jerusalem: The Hebrew University, 1971.

Stahl, A. Language and thought of culturally deprived children in Israel. Tel-Aviv: Otsar Hamoreh, 1977 (Hebrew).

Stubbs, M. Language, schools and classrooms. (second edition). London: Methuen, 1983.

Vidislavsky, D. Syntactical and lexical features of the spoken language of children from Western and Middle-Eastern background. 'Free' Hebrew Linguistics, 1984, 21, 9-27 (Hebrew).

Vigotsky, L. Thought and language. Cambridge, Mass: M.I.T. Press, 1962.

Webb, N. A process-outcome analysis of learning in group and individual settings. Educational Psychologist. 1980, 15, 69-83.

Webb, N. Peer interaction and learning in cooperative small groups. Journal of Educational Psychology. 1982, 74, 642-655.

Webb, N. Student interaction and learning in small groups: A research summary. In: R.Slavin, S.Sharan, et al (Eds.): Learning to cooperate, cooperating to learn. New York: Plenum, 1985, 147-172.

Wells, G. The meaning makers: Children learning language and using language to learn. Portsmouth, New Hampshire: Heinemann, 1986.

Widdowson, H. Teaching language as communication. Oxford: Oxford University Press, 1978.

Wilkinson, L. and Calculator, S. Effective speakers: Using language to request and obtain information and action in the classroom. In: L. Wilkinson (Ed.), Communicating in the classroom, New York: Academic Press, 1982.

Williams, F. (Ed.), Language and poverty. Chicago: Markham, 1970.

APPENDIX

Table 23:   Means and SDs of pretest and post-test scores on low and high level questions of classes that studied History with the Group-Investigation or Whole-Class method.

| | | Low-level | | High-Level | | |
		pre	post	pre	post	N
Class			Group Investigation			
1	M	10.69	39.57	10.97	21.60	35
	SD	6.23	6.17	5.52	4.89	
2	M	12.03	32.47	7.38	19.75	32
	SD	4.55	8.47	5.31	8.91	
3	M	11.31	34.47	9.72	21.79	39
	SD	4.79	8.86	5.17	8.19	
4	M	8.32	41.11	6.24	22.24	38
	SD	4.50	5.42	5.14	3.93	
5	M	9.35	36.19	11.08	26.30	37
	SD	6.02	7.20	5.12	5.14	
			Whole-Class			
1	M	11.92	16.60	5.82	7.19	27
	SD	5.10	6.01	5.43	4.92	
2	M	12.22	30.39	8.56	16.53	36
	SD	8.99	8.07	7.13	8.86	
3	M	7.79	21.36	6.82	15.46	33
	SD	4.72	7.27	4.90	5.76	

Table 24: Means and SDs of pretest and post-test scores on low and high-level questions of classes that studied Geography with the Group-Investigation or Whole-Class methods.

		Low-Level		High-Level		
		pre	post	pre	post	N
Class		Group-Investigation				
1	M	6.41	34.65	8.85	23.62	34
	SD	5.55	12.97	4.89	7.10	
2	M	9.22	33.72	8.33	24.86	36
	SD	6.71	8.24	5.76	5.72	
3	M	8.51	34.30	8.16	27.49	37
	SD	4.13	7.30	3.89	4.98	
4	M	7.30	37.78	8.68	26.60	37
	SD	7.87	7.31	5.27	5.22	
5	M	3.66	38.09	3.47	28.00	32
	SD	2.78	6.62	2.21	4.82	
		Whole-Class				
2	M	6.24	23.16	5.19	18.41	37
	SD	5.26	8.01	3.92	7.88	
3	M	9.22	28.22	9.53	17.56	36
	SD	9.74	10.72	5.23	8.27	

The data in Tables 23 and 24 were analyzed by analyses of covariance with repeated measures, where Classes were nested in Methods, pre- and post-test scores were used as repeated measures, and father's education served as the co-variate. Analysis of the Low-level questions on the achievement test in History (Table 23) yielded significant interaction effects for Method x Time of Test ($F=267.00$, $p<.001$), Class x Time ($F=133.59$, $p<.001$). Significant interactions emerged for Method x Time ($F=271.67$, $p<.001$), Class x Time ($F=68.18$, $p<.001$) and Method x Class x Time ($F=136.79$, $p<.001$).

Findings from the same kind of analyses of the Geography scores (Table 24) parallel those found for History, namely: significant interactions in the analysis of data from the Low-level questions were found for Method x Time ($F=240.08$, $p<.001$), Class x Time ($F=61.71$, $p<.001$), and Method x Class x Time ($F=242.93$, $p<.001$). Results for the High-level questions were: Method x Time ($F=240.24$, $p<.001$), Class x Time ($F=61.71$, $p<.001$), Method x Class x Time ($F=243.71$, $p<.001$).

The Group Investigation method promoted significantly higher levels of student achievement than the Whole Class method even though there were significant differences in achievement between classes. No class taught with the Whole Class approach achieved as high a score on these tests, on both Low and High level questions, as did any class taught with the Group Investigation method.

Table 25: <u>Pearson Correlations among all Dependent Measures</u>

	Co	Cf	CS	FI	TS	MWT	N	LG	HG	LH
HH	.11	-.02	-.05	-.10	-.04	-.01	-.04	.43	.32	.58
LH	.27	-.04	.12	.05	.03	-.11	.05	.64	.39	
HG	-.13	-.12	-.18	-.22	-.12	.00	-.21	.62		
LG	.15	.09	.05	.02	.08	-.04	.02			
N	.74	.49	.70	.50	.52	-.70				
MWT	-.42	-.37	-.43	-.26	-.03					
TS	.53	.18	.57	.57						
FI	.38	.30	.83							
CS	.53	.33								
Cf	.47									

Co=Cooperative Acts

Cf=Conflicted or
    Competitive Acts

CS=Cognitive Strategies

FI=Focused Interactions

TS=Turns of Speech

MWT=Mean Number of Words per Turn

N=Number of Words spoken

LG=Low-Level Questions, Geography

HG=High-Level Questions, Geography

LH=Low-Level Questions, History

HH=High-Level Questions, History

175

The correlations in Table 25 reveal three distinct groupings of variables in terms of their inter-relationships. Three (CS, FI, TS) out of the four measures of verbal behavior are related (correlation range from .47 to .83), as are the four measures of achievement (LG, HG, LH and HH) whose inter-correlations range from .32 to .64. The verbal measures are also related to cooperative and competitive acts (Co, Cf) which, like the verbal and social measures, were derived from the tape-recorded discussions. Cooperative acts related, albeit at low levels (.11, .15, .27), to three achievement measures, but not to a fourth (Co and HH correlate at -.13). See Table 22 (page 99) for the regression analyses indicating the amount of variance in the achievement scores accounted for by the social and verbal variables measured during the 30-minute discussions.